THE CHOICE
OF WAGE COMPARISONS

1960 Award Winner

THE FORD FOUNDATION DOCTORAL DISSERTATION SERIES

*A dissertation submitted in partial fulfillment
of the requirements for the degree of Doctor
of Philosophy at the University of Michigan*

1959 Award Winners

Kalman J. Cohen
Computer Models of the Shoe, Leather, Hide Sequence
Dissertation submitted to Graduate School of Industrial Administration,
Carnegie Institute of Technology

Present Position: Associate Professor of Economics and Industrial Administration, Graduate School of Industrial Administration, Carnegie
Institute of Technology

Bob R. Holdren
*The Structure of a Retail Market and the Market
Behavior of Retail Units*
Dissertation submitted to Department of Economics, Yale University

Present Position: Assistant Professor of Economics, Iowa State University,
Ames, Iowa

Frank Proschan
*Polya Type Distributions in Renewal Theory, with an
Application to an Inventory Problem*
Dissertation submitted to Department of Statistics, Stanford University

Present Position: Staff Member, Mathematics Laboratory, Boeing Scientific Research Laboratories

Andrew C. Stedry
Budget Control and Cost Behavior
Dissertation submitted to Graduate School of Industrial Administration,
Carnegie Institute of Technology

Present Position: Second Lieutenant, United States Army, Operational
Mathematics Branch, Research & Engineering Div.

Victor H. Vroom
Some Personality Determinants of the Effects of Participation
Dissertation submitted to Department of Psychology, University of
Michigan

Present Position: Assistant Professor of Psychology, University of
Pennsylvania

THE CHOICE

OF WAGE COMPARISONS

MARTIN PATCHEN

*Department of Social Psychology,
University of Michigan*

1961

P R E N T I C E - H A L L ,   I N C .

Englewood Cliffs, N. J.

© — *1961 by* PRENTICE-HALL, INC.
Englewood Cliffs, N. J.

L. C. Catalog Card Number: 61-11081

• *Printed in the United States of America*
13339—C

Foreword

This volume is one of five doctoral dissertations selected for publication in the second annual Doctoral Dissertation Competition sponsored by the Program in Economic Development and Administration of The Ford Foundation. The winning dissertations were completed during the academic year 1959–60 by doctoral candidates in business administration, in the social sciences and other fields relevant to the study of problems of business.

The dissertation competition is intended to generalize standards of excellence in research on business by graduate students. It should give widespread professional recognition to persons recently awarded doctorates in business whose dissertation research is especially distinguished by its analytical content and strong roots in underlying disciplines. It is also intended to give recognition to a select number of persons outside business schools who in the their doctoral dissertations pursued with distinction interests relevant to the field of business.

The dissertations selected include, in addition to Dr. Patchen's monograph:

Decentralization of Authority in a Bureaucracy
        Bernard H. Baum
        Department of Sociology
        University of Chicago

The Distribution of Automobiles, An Economic Analysis of the Franchise System
        Bedros Peter Pashigian
        Department of Economics
        Massachusetts Institute of Technology

Marketing in an Underdeveloped Economy: The North Indian Sugar Industry
        Leon V. Hirsch
        Graduate School of Business Administration
        Harvard University

A Heuristic Program for Assembly Line Balancing
Fred M. Tonge
Graduate School of Industrial Administration
Carnegie Institute of Technology

In the first year of the competition four of the five dissertations selected made extensive use of mathematical and statistical tools. This may have led some to the mistaken impression that mathematically-oriented dissertations are unduly favored in the selection process. The results of the second year's competition should serve to correct any such misapprehension. Four of the five dissertations published this year are largely non-mathematical, thus underscoring our conviction that many disciplines, including mathematics, can make important contributions to rigorous business research.

On behalf of The Ford Foundation, I wish to express my gratitude to the Editorial Committee for the care and thought its members devoted to the selection process. The same scholars who served on the Committee for the first year's competition gave us the benefit of their experience by serving a second year. They are: Professors Robert Ferber of the University of Illinois, Sherman J. Maisel of the University of California (Berkeley), and William Foote Whyte of Cornell University.

As in the first year, the Editorial Committee's task was considerably lightened by the assistance of ten readers, experts in the wide range of disciplines covered in the Competition, who carefully screened each of the dissertations submitted. The Foundation joins the Committee in acknowledging their debt to Professors Austin C. Hoggatt, Julius Margolis and Lyman W. Porter of the University of California (Berkeley), Richard M. Cyert of the Carnegie Institute of Technology, Harry V. Roberts of the University of Chicago, Frank Miller and Henry Landsberger of Cornell University, Myron J. Gordon of the Massachusetts Institute of Technology, Samuel Goldberg of Oberlin College, and Robert B. Fetter of Yale University, for serving as readers in the second year of the competition.

Finally, my colleagues and I wish to acknowledge the substantial contribution of Prentice-Hall, Inc., to the publication and distribution of the selected dissertations.

THOMAS H. CARROLL
VICE PRESIDENT
THE FORD FOUNDATION

New York, New York
December, 1960

Preface

This study was carried out under the auspices of the Organization Behavior and Organization Change Program of the Institute for Social Research. I am grateful for the freedom given me within this program to plan and carry out this study, as well as for the assistance of many persons within the Institute. I owe a special debt of gratitute to Mrs. Carol Slater, acting director of the study, who contributed generously of her time and thought, especially during the planning stages of the research. I am also indebted for technical help at various stages of the study to Dr. Floyd C. Mann, Dr. Donald C. Pelz, Dr. Arnold S. Tannenbaum, and Mr. Edwin H. Blakelock, and for clerical assistance to Mrs. Margaret Nierenberg and Mrs. Betty Sears—all of the Institute for Social Research.

I would like to thank the members of my doctoral committee for their advice and assistance. I am especially grateful to the committee chairman, Dr. Theodore M. Newcomb, for his help at all stages of this research and for his continual willingness to be of service, regardless of personal inconvenience to himself.

I would like to acknowledge too the generous cooperation of the management of the refinery at which this research was carried out, and of the men whom we interviewed at the refinery. Without their interest and aid, this study could not, of course, have been successfully completed.

I wish, finally, to thank my wife, Susan Patchen, for her clerical help, and for her constant interest and encouragement in this research.

MARTIN PATCHEN

Contents

ix

CHAPTER 4

THE RELATION BETWEEN DISSONANCE
AND SATISFACTION   *35*

CHAPTER 5

RELATIVE PAY AND ABSOLUTE PAY   *49*

CHAPTER 6

MOBILITY CHANCES   *58*

CHAPTER 7

ACCEPTANCE OF PERSONAL RESPONSIBILITY   *88*

CHAPTER 8

SOCIAL INFLUENCES 95

CHAPTER 9

SNMMARY AND CONCLUSIONS 102

APPENDIX A

RESPONSE DISTRIBUTIONS NOT REPORTED ELSEWHERE 113

APPENDIX B

PAY RATE DISTRIBUTION 119

APPENDIX C

METHODOLOGICAL NOTE 120

BIBLIOGRAPHY 122

CHAPTER 1

Some Previous Work and
Some Remaining Problems

1.1. Previous Work on Social Comparisons

There has long been a recognition in the social sciences that an individual's view of himself and of the world about him are shaped by his social frame of reference.

The social philosophers and early sociologists of the late nineteenth and early twentieth centuries emphasized the importance of group influences on the individual. Prominent contributors to this early sociological thought were Summer (1906), in his discussion of group folkways and mores; Cooley (1902), in his description of primary group influences on the individual; Durkheim (1897, 1912), in his conception of the overpowering impact of group affiliations on individual religious behavior and on suicide rates; and Mead (1934), in his analysis of the ways in which the very mind and self-concept of the individual are formed through his interactions with "significant others."

In general psychology, interest in the influence of group standards on individuals arose in connection with work on "level of aspiration" phenomena. Chapman and Volkmann (1939), Hilgard, Sait, and Magaret (1940), and McIntosh (1942) showed

1

in the laboratory that the goals which people set for themselves in a variety of tasks are raised or lowered according to the relative standing of pertinent social groups.

At about the same time, social psychologists, drawing on both the disciplines of sociology and psychology, began to focus increased attention on the subject of reference group standards. Hyman (1942) studied experimentally the way in which a person's judgment of his status on a number of criteria (e.g., intellectual, cultural, economic) varied as the social comparisons were varied. A number of studies indicated the important effect of reference groups on perceptual judgments. Especially noteworthy is Sherif's classic study with the autokinetic effect (1935), in which individual judgments in an ambiguous situation were shown to follow closely the guidelines set by others' judgments. Reference group standards were shown also to exert a marked effect on social attitudes. Prominent among relevant studies in this area is Newcomb's careful tracing of a change among college girls toward more "liberal" socio-economic views as they came more under the influence of the standards of their college community (1943). Discussions of the nature and effects of reference group standards in the books by Newcomb and by Sherif (1936) furthered understanding of these subjects and stimulated further inquiry.

Sociologists, despite the fact that the fathers of the discipline had given prominent attention to the subject of group influences on the individual, gave only sporadic attention to the questions which remained unanswered in this area until the publication of *The American Soldier* volumes (1949–50) following World War II. This wartime research showed dramatically that the attitudes of men toward Army procedures and toward their own position in the Army, their self-evaluations, and their satisfactions, could not be explained merely by knowing their objective conditions or their actual membership groups (e.g., what Army branch a man was in). In order to account for a number of puzzling and paradoxical findings, Stouffer and his associates utilized the concept of "relative deprivation." They were able to find order in their data by assuming that many differences in attitudes were due to the fact that different categories of men compared themselves to different groups.

The implications for sociological theory of *The American Soldier,* as well as the theoretical problems which these volumes raised, have been discussed by Merton and Kitt (1950). Among the points raised by their essay is the importance of being able to understand and predict which of many possible reference groups an individual will choose. They formulate the problem in this way:

> Why will A, in one situation, compare himself with B, and in another with C? Or more concretely and illustratively: when do workers compare their lot with that of fellow workers in close association, and when with others of markedly different status? Which aspects of social structure and which psychological processes limit the range of individuals and groups regarded as pertinent frames of reference? It is this type of problem—the processes shaping the selection of reference groups—that stands in most conspicuous need of research [1950, p. 69].

Some interesting qualitative materials pertinent to these questions were gathered in the early series of studies by Hyman (1942). In intensive "clinical" interviews with thirty-one subjects from a variety of occupations, he asked each subject quite directly what group of people he compared himself with on each of thirteen dimensions of status. The status dimensions covered a wide range, from economic position to athletic ability. Hyman notes that comparison persons were sometimes chosen on the basis of their similarity to the comparer and sometimes on the basis of their contrast to the comparer. He states:

> The reference individuals in many cases are chosen by virtue of similarity to the subject, proximity to him in life situation, or as the result of objective facts which facilitate such comparison. The term *affinity* is used to cover such instances.

> Other reference individuals are chosen for comparisons of status by virtue of contrast with the subject's status. They are so different from him that they stand out as sources for comparison [1942, p. 27].

Hyman also discusses the motivational basis for specific comparisons, concluding that comparison to those on a lower level sometimes appears to serve the purpose of inflating the comparer's own status, while comparisons to those on a higher level may "operate via identification, rationalization, or compensation by the use of an alternative reference group, so as not to cause depreciation in status" (1942, p. 25).

Although Hyman's material is provocative, there is no attempt at this early exploratory stage to specify the conditions under which persons will choose comparisons on a higher or lower level, nor when comparisons on one dimension will be to those similar or different on other relevant dimensions.

Merton and Kitt hypothesize an answer to the latter question. After making much of the distinction between comparative reference groups of the same social status and those of different social status, they suggest nevertheless that

> ... some similarity in status attributes between the individual and the reference group must be perceived or imagined in order for the comparison to occur at all. Once this minimal similarity obtains, other similarities and differences pertinent to the situation will provide the context for shaping evaluations [1950, p. 61].

In the work which followed the stimulating Merton-Kitt essay, the research of Turner (1955) provides some evidence that dissimilarity, rather than similarity, may be a crucial factor in determining comparisons. He found that while mobile men usually compared themselves to equal-status persons on matters of morality, they were likely to compare themselves to those of superior status in judging their occupational success. Turner, who used a very indirect method of determining the relevance of certain pre-chosen reference groups, also found that specific groups have different relevance as comparisons in different areas of judgment.

A small number of other studies by sociologists concerning the choice of reference groups have also followed *The American Soldier* volumes and the commentaries on that work. Kaplan (1955), studying voting behavior, found primary groups to be more important than social categories (e.g., religious affiliation) as reference groups. He suggests that primary groups mediate the influence of the broader social categories. Stern and Keller (1953) asked a sample of Frenchmen what they regarded as a "satisfactory standard of living" and coded out spontaneous group references. They distinguished ten kinds of group references, among which the most frequent were social class, family, and occupational group—in that order.

Aside from the work of the sociologists, the most important recent work concerning the choice of social comparisons has emerged from data on small group processes, as analyzed by Festinger (1955). Festinger has not studied the choice of comparisons directly, but, on the basis of a large number of studies concerning communication, influence, attraction and rejection, and level of aspiration within groups, he has elaborated a number of formally derived and related hypotheses constituting "a theory of social comparison processes." Most pertinent for our present concerns are the following:

> Given a range of possible persons for comparison, someone close to one's own ability or opinion will be chosen for comparison [1955, p. 167].

> If persons who are very divergent from one's own opinion or ability are perceived as different from oneself on *attributes consistent with the divergence,* the tendency to narrow the range of comparability becomes stronger [1955, p. 180].

Festinger bases his theory on a hypothesized "drive" of the individual "to evaluate his opinions and his abilities." The relevance of the theory to the evaluation of personal characteristics other than opinions and abilities (e.g., social status, treatment by others, moral goodness) is not made clear by Festinger.

Finally, in our review of work in the area of social comparisons, a theoretical contribution by Kelley (1952) is important to note. Kelley has pointed to the distinction between the function of a reference group as a norm-setter for the individual, as opposed to its function as a standard of comparison. That the two functions do not necessarily go together is made plain by the simple example of a child who is urged by his parents to do as well in school as the bright Jones children. His parents are the group whose norms he accepts. The Jones children are the comparison group specified by those norms.

1.2. Remaining Problems

The problem put by Merton and Kitt—in short, what factors determine to whom a person will compare himself—is the central problem of the present research. Our review of the literature indicates that only a beginning has been made toward answering this question.

Most of the relevant studies cited were largely exploratory, with little or no systematic hypothesis-testing. The only coherent theory of social comparisons is that advanced by Festinger. But as we have seen, his hypotheses are derived indirectly from phenomena related to comparisons and have not been directly tested.

The common-sense question, "To whom does a man compare himself?" has, in the studies cited, involved two more precise questions. These are:

1. When does someone compare himself to others who are higher, lower, or equal on the dimension of comparison?
2. When does someone compare himself to others who are of higher, lower, or equal status on additional attributes relevant to the dimension of comparison?

The distinction between these two questions has usually not been made clear, and has sometimes resulted in conceptual confusion.

In answer to the first question there is little knowledge at present. Hyman presents striking illustrations of "motivated" comparisons to both those higher and lower on the status dimension being judged, but his exploratory work gives few clues to the reasons why one man should be motivated to compare "up" and another motivated to compare "down." *The American Soldier* investigators give little attention to this question, seeming to assume that whether a man turns out to be comparing to those higher or lower than himself is rather accidental, depending on what his particular reference group happens to be. Festinger has little to say on this subject, assuming "pressures for uniformity" within the group. Turner, however, suggests that upwardly mobile persons generally wish to be *above* the average for their groups, which would dispose them to compare themselves to persons who are inferior in some way. Turner found an exception to this generalization, though, when his upwardly mobile subjects tended to use those in a *superior* position as a reference group for occupational success.

On the second major question distinquished here—under what conditions persons of generally dissimilar status will be chosen as comparisons on a particular dimension—there is also little knowledge. Festinger's hypotheses, as quoted above, state essentially that an individual will compare himself to those close to him, not only on the dimension being judged, but on other related dimensions as well. However, the data of Hyman and others cited show that people will often compare themselves to others who are, in general, markedly different from themselves. In addition, Merton and Kitt point to the problem of determining when comparisons on a given dimension will be made to those who are generally similar or generally dissimilar in other ways.

Finally, there emerges the interesting question of the relation between the "direction" of comparison (to those higher, equal, or lower on the dimension judged) and the general status characteristics of the comparison persons. Specifically, questions like these arise: When a person compares himself to someone higher than himself (on the dimension judged), under what conditions will this "upward" comparison be to someone similar to himself in other ways? When a person compares himself to someone lower than himself (on the dimension judged), when will the comparison person be someone who is similar to the comparer in other relevant ways?

It is with understanding such problems—the "direction" of social comparisons, the status of comparison persons chosen, and the relation between the two—that the present work is concerned.

Chapter 2 will outline a theoretical approach to these problems and state a number of hypotheses derived from this approach. Chapter 3 will describe the operations and procedures used to test these hypotheses. Chapters 4 through 8 will present the results of this investigation, and Chapter 9 will present a summary of the research and suggest the conclusions which may be drawn from it.

Theory and Hypotheses

2.1. Nature of the Comparison Process

On the basis of exploratory interviews at the present research site, it seems useful to conceptualize the comparison process as follows: In trying to judge his position on some dimension, an individual compares his standing on this dimension to the standing of another person. At the same time, he compares himself to the other person(s) on some other dimension or dimensions which are related to standing on the first dimension.

In the present research, individuals are asked to compare themselves to others on the dimension of earnings. But these comparisons on pay cannot be made in a cognitive vacuum. Such comparisons become meaningful to the individual only when he also compares himself to others on dimensions which are believed to be bases of pay (e.g., skill, seniority, education), or which are otherwise related to job pay (e.g., how interesting others' jobs appear to be).

In effect, the individual makes a cognitive relation of the following type:

$$(1) \quad \frac{\text{my pay}}{\text{his (their) pay}} \quad \text{compared to} \quad \frac{\text{my position on dimensions related to pay}}{\text{his (their) position on dimensions related to pay}}$$

We may define conceptually a *perceived consonant comparison* as one in which the comparer perceives one side of this relation (the ratio of one's own pay to another's pay) as congruent with, or appropriate to, the other side of the relation (i.e., the ratio of one's own position on related dimensions to another's position on related dimensions). Similarly, a *perceived dissonant comparison* is defined as one in which the comparer perceives the ratio on one side of the relation as incongruent with, or inappropriate to, the ratio on the other side of the relation.[1]

It is also possible to distinguish among comparisons according to the degree of objective dissonance present. Some comparisons—e.g., to men of the same education and age as the comparer who are earning more than he—provide more objective bases for the comparer to perceive dissonance than do other comparisons (e.g., to older men with more schooling who are earning more than he). We define *objectively consonant comparisons* as those in which the ratio of the comparer's position on dimensions relevant to pay to another's position on these relevant dimensions is by most persons in this culture to be congruent with, or appropriate to, the ratio of their earnings. *Objectively dissonant comparisons* are, similarly, defined as those in which the ratio of the two persons' positions on dimensions relevant to pay is culturally considered incongruent with, or inappropriate to, the ratio of their earnings.

2.2. Dissonance and Satisfaction

It would be expected that a man who perceives a wage comparison to be consonant (i.e., that the wage difference is ap-

---

[1] The term "dissonance" is used in the same sense as Festinger uses it (1957, pp. 13–15). Although the present conceptual framework was developed entirely independently of Festinger's work, it seemed better to adopt his widely known terminology than to introduce new terminology.

propriate to, or "fits with," other differences) has little basis to be dissatisfied with the comparison. He perceives that "justice is being done" and is therefore likely to be satisfied with the comparison.

A man who perceives a dissonant comparison—when the difference in earnings is too much in favor of the comparison person because it does not "fit" with other relevant differences between the men—thereby has a basis for dissatisfaction. The comparer's perception that he is, compared to the other person, earning less than he legitimately "should," is likely to make him angry or ashamed.

Another type of dissonance, that in favor of the comparer, is also possible but will be given only brief attention in this research. The term "dissonant comparison" will be used to refer to dissonance in favor of the comparison person, unless otherwise specified.

2.3. Types of Comparisons Which Result in Consonance or Dissonance

From the preceding general description of the comparison process, it is apparent that the following kinds of pay comparisons will be perceived as *consonant:*

1. Comparison to someone earning less—who is appropriately inferior on dimensions related to pay but not so inferior that the difference in earnings should be even greater,
2. Comparison to someone earning more—who is appropriately superior on dimensions related to pay,
3. Comparison to someone earning the same—who is similar to the comparer on dimensions related to pay.

There are likewise a number of kinds of pay comparisons which will be perceived as *dissonant.* These include:

4. Comparison to someone earning more—who is similar on dimensions related to pay,

5. Comparison to someone earning less—but who is so far inferior on dimensions related to pay that the difference in earnings should be even greater,

6. Comparison to someone earning the same—who is inferior on attributes related to pay.

In the present study, respondents were asked to compare themselves to persons whose earnings are different from their own. Therefore, comparison types 3 and 6 above do not occur in the data.

Of the two consonant comparison types possible in this research (types 1 and 2), type 1 (comparisons to those earning less than oneself) are more likely to be satisfying to the comparer. It is probably easier to find satisfaction in earning more than another than in seeing oneself as appropriately inferior. Even though one's lower pay may be seen as "appropriate," the fact of inferiority can never inspire much pleasure. Another reason why, in the present research, comparisons to lower-earners are most likely to be satisfying is that these low-earners are sometimes of similar status as the comparer. Such downward comparisons are, in a sense, better than satisfactory for the comparer. It should be reiterated, however, that many upward comparisons, which are objectively consonant, and which are perceived as such, will also be viewed as satisfactory.

Of the two major types of dissonant comparisons possible in our data (types 4 and 5), type 4 (comparisons to those inappropriately earning more) may be expected to be experienced as unsatisfactory more frequently and more strongly. It is probably easier to be dissatisfied about earning less than about earning only a little more than someone else. Being superior to another in wages is, in itself, a pleasant state of affairs, even though one may perceive that the difference should be even greater.

Having identified specific types of consonant and dissonant wage comparisons, we can derive some hypotheses from our conceptual scheme. If our general description of the relation between dissonance and dissatisfaction is correct, we would expect the following hypotheses to be supported:

Hypothesis 1. Wage comparisons which are objectively dissonant will be judged as unsatisfactory by the person who chooses such comparisons.

Specifically:
Hypothesis 1A. Men who choose "upward" wage comparisons who are similar in status (same occupational level, same place of work, or same family) will more often be dissatisfied with such comparisons than will men who choose upward comparisons of different status.

Hypothesis 2. Men who are satisfied with specific wage comparisons will explain their satisfaction in terms of a consonance between relative wage standing and relative standing on attributes related to pay; men who are dissatisfied with specific comparisons will explain their dissatisfaction in terms of a dissonance between relative wage standing and standing on attributes relevant to pay.

2.4. Potential Dissonance

So far, consonant and dissonant comparisons have been discussed as they apply to the comparer's present position. However, there is implicit in many types of comparisons—and this appears to be true of comparisons on pay—an awareness of *potential* dissonance. In the case of comparisons on pay, the question is: "Will I make as much in the future as he's making now, and, if not, would this be right?" Where the individual perceives a specific comparison as consonant at present, it is nevertheless of great importance to know whether he perceives potential dissonance (i.e., whether he would be satisfied if the difference in pay remained the same as it is now). In many cases he would not. The potential dissonance in the relation usually arises from the fact that he may expect his own position on the secondary dimension to change. For example, the assistant mechanic may believe that, considering the differences now existing between himself and the senior mechanic in skill, seniority, and age, the difference in wages is appropriate. However, he may expect his own qualifications to become more like those of the senior man and thus expect an eventual raise in pay. Moreover, this potential dissonance may be an important aspect of the comparison for him, and we will therefore have to consider it in our analysis.

More formally, potential (or future) consonance or dissonance may be thought of as resulting from the following relation:

$$(2) \qquad \frac{\text{my pay now}}{\text{his (their) pay now}} \quad \text{compared to} \quad \frac{\text{my } \textit{future} \text{ position on dimensions related to pay}}{\text{his (their) present position on dimensions related to pay}}$$

A perceived *potentially consonant comparison* may be defined as one in which the comparer perceives that one side of relation 2 (the ratio of comparer's future position on dimensions related to pay to another's present position on these dimensions) is congruent with, or appropriate to, the other side of the relation (present ratio of their earnings). Similarly, a perceived *potentially dissonant comparison* is defined as one in which the comparer perceives that one side of relation 2 is incongruent with, or inappropriate to, the other side of the relation.

2.5. Motivation toward Satisfaction or Dissatisfaction

So far, we have used our conceptual picture of the comparison process to try to predict the relation between objective and perceived dissonance, on the one hand, and satisfaction with comparisons, on the other.

This, however, is not our main problem. Nor would the conceptual scheme presented be of great use if it merely permitted us to predict the satisfactoriness of a particular kind of comparison. Our central problem is to try to understand and to predict why one particular kind of comparison, rather than another, has been chosen. Of what help in this task is our conceptual picture of the comparison process?

At this point we need to make a crucial assumption. We have argued that satisfaction with a comparison depends on whether the comparison is perceived as consonant or not. But for any individual it is not a matter of indifference whether he perceives the comparisons he makes as consonant or dissonant. If he makes consonant comparisons, he has the satisfaction of feeling that he has achieved his rightful status, has been granted or has achieved what is appropriate for him. All's right with the world —at least as it concerns his standing on this one dimension. However, a presently consonant comparison affords no basis for claiming that one deserves a higher status now, and a comparison which will remain consonant in the future provides no basis for claiming to deserve a higher status in the future.

The person who perceives present dissonance (that which is unfavorable to himself) has to shoulder the burden of anger and frustration and—in some cases—a feeling of failure. However, he has the advantage of being able to tell himself and others that a man like himself really deserves a higher status.

Attention to comparisons which involve present consonance but *future* dissonance provides the individual with the satisfaction of feeling that he merits higher status in the future. In many cases, it may also bring him pleasant anticipations of this higher position. Such a comparison, involving *potential* dissonance, does not place as much strain of anger and frustration on the individual as a comparison involving *present* dissonance. However, unlike the person who focuses on completely consonant comparisons, the individual who focuses on potential dissonance is not enjoying as much the satisfaction deriving from his present adequate status. Moreover, there is probably some anxiety about whether or not dissonance will actually occur in the future (e.g., by his not getting a raise after achieving greater experience and seniority).

In short, it appears that the greatest present satisfaction will follow from perceptions of completely consonant comparisons. However, this contentment is brought at the price of renouncing a claim to a presently (and perhaps future) higher status. The man who perceives dissonance may have to suffer dissatisfaction and even anger, but he has the advantage of feeling that a higher status would be appropriate for him.

The different rewards and punishments associated with different types of comparisons are not, however, equally available to all persons. That is to say, some individuals, by virtue of their objective position, chances for change in position, and so on, will be more likely to derive rewards from one kind of comparison than persons in different circumstances will derive from that particular kind of comparison. Thus, some persons will be more likely to *want* to perceive present or future consonance in comparisons of pay than will others. If this is true, then comparers should be motivated to *choose* comparisons according to whether they are consonant or dissonant. This means that if we know something about the social circumstances of the comparer, and about his resultant motives to be satisfied or dissatisfied with comparisons, we are then in a position to predict whether he will choose consonant or dissonant wage comparisons. Specifically, we should be able to predict (1) whether he will choose comparisons who are earning more or less than himself, and (2) whether he will choose comparisons who are of generally similar or dissimilar status in ways related to pay.

Since dissonance or consonance results from the specific combination of these two factors (i.e., of relative positions on pay, as compared to relative position on other status dimensions), it will be important to consider both of these factors at the same time. In fact, this way of looking at concrete data is one of the primary benefits of the conceptual framework outlined above. The importance of the conceptual approach is, thus, not confined to a theoretical analysis. The hypotheses to be stated later and the operations for testing them rest heavily on the idea of considering *simultaneously* the direction of comparison (relative pay position) and the status characteristics of the comparison person (relative position on the dimensions related to pay).

2.6. Objective Status

Although the motivational forces behind the choice of dissonant or consonant comparisons have been emphasized so far, other conditions affecting the amount of dissonance in comparisons are also considered in the present framework. Specifically, predictions are made concerning the effect of a man's objective wage position, relative to those of like status, on the type of wage comparisons he makes. Besides its importance as a predictor in itself, such data on objective position are important as a control on the effect of more motivationally relevant variables.

Another way of looking at the role of the objective position variable within the general conceptual framework is that there is postulated a two-way causal relationship between dissonance and satisfaction. If, by virtue of his objective position, a man is confronted with dissonant comparisons, he will be dissatisfied. In contrast, if he is motivated to be dissatisfied, he will choose dissonant comparisons from among those available.

2.7. Determinants of Choosing Consonant and Dissonant Comparisons

The next job is to try to predict which men will choose comparisons that they perceive as consonant and which men will choose comparisons that represent dissonance for them.

We will consider the effects of four major variables on the choice of wage comparisons. These are:

1. Objective wage position, relative to those of like status.
2. Mobility chances—both objective and perceived.

3. Perception of personal responsibility for job position.
4. Primary group definitions of the adequacy of his present wages—as reported by the respondent.

Objective Wage Position, Relative to Those of Like Status. It has often been assumed (e.g., by Festinger [1955]) that individuals compare themselves, not to all other persons, but mainly to others who are generally like themselves.

In considering the effects of a man's relative wage position on his choice of pay comparisons, we will accept this assumption. It is accepted here, however, as only a general tendency. The generalization that persons will compare to others "like themselves" in over-all status will hold only under certain conditions.

This argument will be developed at length throughout the rest of this work. For the present, however, we may accept the assumption that under most conditions people will compare their wages to the earnings of those who are like themselves in ways which are culturally considered relevant to standing on earnings.

If this is true, then we should expect those who are doing poorly on wages relative to those like themselves to choose often as comparisons those who are earning more. This would result simply from the fact that most people "like themselves" are earning more. It is apparent also that such comparisons would, according to our conceptual scheme, be dissonant—that is, the difference in pay would not be seen as appropriate to the similarity in general status.

If the assumption of previous work—that people will compare themselves to those like themselves—is generally correct, and if our reasoning from this assumption is also correct, we would expect the following hypothesis to be supported:

Hypothesis 3. Men whose earnings are lower than the earnings of most others who are objectively similar to them on attributes culturally considered relevant to pay, will be more likely than others to choose dissonant wage comparisons. (This will be true regardless of their absolute wage level.)

Specifically:

Hypothesis 3A. They will more often choose as comparisons those who are earning more than themselves.

Hypothesis 3B. When they choose as comparisons those who are earning more than themselves, such comparison persons are likely to be of similar status (in occupational level, place of work, and family).

If hypothesis 3 is correct, we would expect also:

Hypothesis 4. Men whose earnings are lower than the earnings of most persons who are objectively similar to them on attributes culturally considered relevant to pay will, more often than others, be dissatisfied with comparisons to persons who earn more than themselves.

Data bearing on hypotheses 3 and 4 will also provide a test of an important proposition advanced in *The American Soldier* volumes—that relative position is more important than absolute position as a determinant of comparisons and of satisfaction. The reference groups used to assess relative position in these volumes (e.g., other married men, other captains) were assumed, plausibly but often ex post facto, to be important comparison groups. The reference groups used in the present research to measure a man's relative position (i.e., age groups, educational groups, seniority groups, and relatives) were chosen previous to the collection and analysis of data, on the basis of approximately fifty exploratory interviews. Moreover, in the present research, a man's relative wage position has been defined quantitatively, while the wartime researches were based in part on non-quantitative evidence. (For example, in the Army research, it is hard to estimate how much greater status was enjoyed by Negro soldiers in the South than by Negro civilians in the South—a question which was vital to the interpretation of one set of data.) For these reasons, the present research will provide a somewhat more systematic and quantative test of the general propositions advanced by Stouffer and his associates.

A limitation of the present research should be noted, however. When we say that we expect a man to compare himself to others like himself on "attributes culturally considered relevant to pay" we need to be able to specify just which status attributes are considered relevant in any given situation. In the present research, we would need complete information about which status dimensions are seen as relevant for judging the appropriateness of a given pay difference.

This general question constitutes a separate research problem. In the present research, no systematic answer to this question is attempted.

The status dimensions (age, education, seniority, family status) used to compare a man's wages to the wages of others like himself were found in exploratory interviews to be ones which are important in the thinking of the men studied. The actual importance of these status dimensions as a framework for wage comparisons is demonstrated by the data to be presented. However, the question of what other status dimensions are or are not relevant to wage comparisons was not systematically explored.

Mobility Chances. When a man makes a dissonant wage comparison (e.g., to someone like himself who is earning more), this comparison is necessarily accompanied by dissatisfaction and often by unpleasant emotions like anger, frustration, or shame. Festinger states that "the presence of dissonance gives rise to pressures to reduce that dissonance" (1957, p. 263). In the situation of wage comparisons, however, there is reason to predict that there may also be pressures in the opposite direction (i.e., to promote and maintain dissonance) at least in the short run. How great a man's chances are for changing his wage position should make a great difference in his willingness to continue making and, indeed, seeking dissonant comparisons.

The man who is stuck in his present wage position, with little chance for advancement, has much to gain from reducing the dissonance of wage comparisons—either by choosing new comparisons or by reinterpreting previous ones. By reducing dissonance he need no longer feel inferior to those like himself and need no longer have to shoulder the burden of anger, frustration, or shame.

But consider the man who has a chance to move upward in the wage scale. Rather than satisfying himself with the status quo, he may wish to perceive potential dissonance (i.e., that it would be inappropriate for him to remain lower than certain comparison persons in wages). Such potential dissonance would serve to justify and legitimate his claims for advancement. Moreover, rather than being satisfied with his present wage status, it may be pleasant for him to lay advance claim to a prospective higher status.

The upwardly mobile man wants consonance to be re-established, but he wants this to happen through an increase in his wage level, that is, for an equilibrium to be re-established at a higher level. For the present, he may welcome perceptions of present or potential dissonance.

On the basis of this reasoning, the following hypothesis is advanced:

Hypothesis 5. Men who have good chances for upward mobility will be more likely than others to make potentially dissonant wage comparisons. (It is predicted that hypothesis 5 will hold true both when we consider objective mobility chances and perceived mobility chances.)

Specifically, from hypothesis 5 we would predict:

Hypothesis 5A. High mobile men will, more often than low mobile men, choose comparison persons who are earning more than themselves.

Hypothesis 5B. When choosing comparison persons who earn more than themselves, high mobile men will tend to choose others who are now or are potentially similar to themselves (e.g., same occupational level, same place of work, same family). Low mobile men, when they make upward comparisons, will tend to choose men who are dissimilar to themselves on attributes relevant to pay.

Hypothesis 5C. High mobile men, when they are presently satisfied with an upward wage comparison, will, more often than low mobile men, give as a reason for present satisfaction their inferior standing on a dimension on which their position will improve (e.g., seniority).

If hypothesis 5 is correct, we would expect also:

Hypothesis 6. High mobile men will, more often than low mobile men, express dissatisfaction at the prospect of *remaining* below comparison persons in the future.

Responsibility for one's fate. Whether or not a man is willing to permit and continue dissonance in his wage comparisons should depend in part on whether or not he views himself as being personally responsible for such an unsatisfactory state of affairs.

If he sees himself as responsible for his present job position, a dissonant wage comparison will make him feel ashamed. Compared to the other person, he is a failure. For men who accept personal responsibility for their fate, there should, therefore, be strong pressures to avoid such dissonant comparisons.

However, the man who sees himself as merely a victim of forces beyond his control is in a different psychological position. If he is doing poorly, he can blame his bad fortune on others—perhaps on the unfairness of his employer—or on bad luck. Although he may prefer to avoid dissonant comparisons for other reasons (e.g., to avoid getting angry), such comparison can serve to give him a claim to a higher status than he actually enjoys. He may be saying, in effect: "I really deserve to be earning as much as that other fellow."

Although it is assumed that generally the sense of personal responsibility will affect the choice of wage comparisons, it is also possible for the relation to work the other way around. That is, the man who perceives dissonant comparisons may change his perception of personal responsibility to adjust to such comparisons. The essential point is that, whichever comes first, dissonant wage comparisons will not long continue to be made unless a man sees the responsibility for his present position as belonging outside himself.

On the basis of this discussion, the following hypothesis is advanced.

Hypothesis 7. Men who see the responsibility for their occupational position as *not* being their own will be more likely than others to choose dissonant wage comparisons.

Specifically:

Hypothesis 7A. "Non-responsible" men will, more often than "responsible" men, choose comparison persons who are earning more than themselves.

Hypothesis 7B. When choosing comparison persons who earn more, "non-responsible" men will, more often than "responsible" men choose persons of similar status (same occupational level, same place of work, or same family).

If hypothesis 7 is correct, we would expect also:

Hypothesis 8. "Non-responsible" men will, more often than "responsible" men, be dissatisfied with upward wage comparisons.

Social Influences. The kinds of wage comparisons a man chooses should also be influenced by what others—especially important others—say to him about his wages. If persons in his family, co-workers, or friends say that he is earning less than is appropriate for him, his attention will be called to objectively dissonant wage comparisons. Moreover, he will be encouraged to see otherwise ambiguous comparisons as dissonant, since there is social backing for such perceptions. Such social definitions of dissonance probably also serve to goad the individual on to try to remedy actual dissonance. (It will be noted that, following Kelley, this discussion implies a distinction between the membership or normative groups, which establish competitive standards for the individual, and the comparison groups or persons specified as standards.)

The effects of social influences should be most evident when the individual is exposed to the assertion that he "deserves" to earn more, or at least where no blame is attached to him for his relatively low position. It is such "non-blaming" social influences that are being investigated in the present research.

The following hypothesis regarding the effect of social pressures is advanced:

Hypothesis 9. Men who are told by others that they deserve to be earning more will more often choose dissonant comparisons.

Specifically:
Hypothesis 9A. They will, more often than men not exposed to such influences, choose comparison persons who earn more than themselves.

Hypothesis 9B. When they choose comparison persons who earn more than themselves, they will, more often than men not exposed to such influences, choose men of similar status (same occupational level, same place of work, or same family).

If hypothesis 9 is correct, we would expect also:
Hypothesis 10. Men who are told by others that they deserve higher earnings will, more often than those not exposed to such influences, be dissatisfied with upward wage comparisons.

2.8. Downward Comparisons

Many of the hypotheses presented so far have concerned upward comparisons (i.e., those earning more). This is because upward comparisons may be either consonant or dissonant. Downward comparisons—to those earning less—are, in the present data, almost never dissonant, and therefore do not serve to test the hypotheses concerning the occurrence of dissonance.

It is possible, theoretically, to differentiate downward comparisons according to whether they are merely consonant or whether they are "favorably dissonant," or more than satisfactory. We might expect, for example, that non-mobile men, anxious to justify their present status, would be more likely to choose downward wage comparisons who are like themselves in other respects. These would be "favorably dissonant" comparisons.

Favorable dissonance is not, however, a major focus of the present research. Moreover, our data bearing on this phenomenon are limited. Thus it will receive little attention in this research.

2.9. Summary

We have outlined a conception of the wage comparison process which focuses on the relation of wage differences to other relevant differences between individuals. Comparisons in which the wage difference is seen by the comparer as inappropriate to other differences between the individuals were labeled "perceived dissonant comparisons." Comparisons in which the objective differences between the individuals are culturally inappropriate to the wage difference (and therefore likely to lead to perceived dissonance) were labeled "objectively dissonant comparisons."

The psychological advantages and disadvantages of the choice of consonant and of dissonant comparisons were discussed. Consonant comparisons were described as those providing the individual with the comfortable, satisfied feeling that he is doing as well as a man like himself should be expected to do. Dissonant comparisons were described as causing the individual to endure anger and frustration, but also as offering him a means to claim a higher wage status. It was predicted that individuals will differ in their motivations to choose dissonant or consonant comparisons, depending on their mobility chances, on their acceptance of personal responsibility for their fate, and on the social influences they experience. The objective factors that make dissonant comparisons more or less perceptually prominent—especially men's wage position relative to others like themselves—were also discussed. Ten hypotheses, based on the discussion in this chapter, were stated.

CHAPTER 3

Operations

3.1. Description of the Site

The research reported here was conducted by the Survey Research Center [1] as part of a larger study of job and life satisfactions at a refinery of the "Atlas Oil Company" of Canada.[2] The refinery is located in a small city of approximately 40,000 population, near the United States border. There are about 1,500 non-supervisory employees working at the refinery. All employees, except a few office workers, are male. The majority of the men are of English or Scottish extraction. Almost all of them are married, and the great majority have children.

The largest group (34 per cent) work at traditional trades, like pipe-fitter, mason, or machinist, in the task of maintaining refinery equipment. Another large group of men (31 per cent) control and regulate the actual production of oil—jobs which require the watching and adjusting of control dials as well as related tasks. Smaller groups of men work at assembly-line jobs —mainly at packaging and manufacturing oil drums (15 per cent), at the testing laboratory (6 per cent), at common labor

---

[1] The writer was an assistant director of this study.

[2] The name of the oil company used in this study is fictitious, and any resemblance to the name of a real company is purely coincidental.

and janitorial work (8 per cent), and at other miscellaneous jobs, like driving trucks (6 per cent).

There is no union at the refinery, although many men in the same area, working in related industries, are unionized. The men at the refinery are represented in negotiations with the management by workers elected to the "Joint Industrial Council." The company has a reputation for paying good wages—often higher than in unionized refineries. In addition, there is an extensive program of company benefits which covers such areas as pensions and sickness and accident payments.

At the time the study was made, the company had recently embarked on an extensive training program to upgrade the skills, and thereby also, the pay and prestige of many of their non-supervisory workers. This training program created an opportunity for men to climb in three or four years an occupational ladder which usually had taken older men twenty or more years of experience and seniority to scale. The training program had been met with enthusiasm by those men who were eligible for it. However, training had been offered in only some—not all—specializations, and even in those trades where it was offered, not all men had the educational (or intellectual) qualifications to enter and complete the training. Informants reported, however, that nearly all men who were genuinely eligible took advantage of the opportunity the training program offered.

3.2. Research Procedures

During the months of May to July, 1958, following exploratory and pretest interviews by the research staff, a team of professional female interviewers interviewed at the refinery a one-third sample of male non-supervisory workers. This sample was stratified by occupational groups and by pay level, with the sample chosen from each group proportional to the size of that group. Of an original sample of 541 men, there were twenty-nine men, or 5.4 per cent, who could not be reached for interviewing

—for such reasons as their being on vacation, being ill, or having retired. There were twenty-two men, or 4.1 per cent, who refused to be interviewed. The number of men included in the final sample was 489, or 90.5 per cent of the original sample.

Respondents were first interviewed for an average of about forty-five minutes, and then were asked to fill out a fixed-alternative questionnaire in the presence of the interviewer.

3.3. Measures

During the interview, the respondent was told: "Now I'd like to ask you a few questions about how your earnings compare with the wages of other people you know about. Who would be someone either here at Atlas or outside the refinery whose yearly earnings are *different* from yours?" [3] After one comparison person was named and identified as to kind of work, the respondent was asked: "Who would be someone else whose yearly earnings are different from yours?" For each of the two comparison persons, the following information is available:

A. *Direction of comparison.* The respondent (R) was asked: "Is he earning more or less than you are right now?"

B. *Occupational level of comparison person.* Responses concerning the type of work done by the comparison persons, as described by R, were coded into the following categories:

1. Professional
2. Proprietor of own business; manager
3. Clerical or sales
4. Foreman (blue-collar supervisory)
5. Blue-collar non-supervisory; skilled and semiskilled, including skilled and semiskilled service workers

---

[3] This rather indirect way of obtaining wage comparisons was adopted after more direct questions caused resentment and defensiveness among some respondents during exploratory interviews. Since time pressure permitted only two comparisons to be obtained and probed, comparisons only to those with *different* earnings were asked for. This restriction was intended to maximize the chances for dissonant comparisons to be chosen.

6. Farm owner or farm worker
7. Unskilled labor including unskilled service workers
8. Unemployed
9. Blue-collar, level of skill and supervision not indicated
10. Other occupation
11. Respondent does not mention comparison person's occupation or does not know this person's occupation

C. *Place of work of comparison person.* Although place of work was not explicitly asked for, it was possible to code 74.4 per cent of the descriptions of comparison persons according to whether or not each worked in the same company as the respondent.

D. *Whether comparison person is a close relative.* Respondents were not asked directly whether the comparison persons they chose were relatives. However, it was possible from the descriptions of comparison persons to code whether or not each was indicated to be a close relative of the respondent. Close relatives were defined as brother, son, father, sister, daughter, mother, and corresponding in-law relations. There may have been a few cases where a close relationship existed but was not indicated, and thus was not coded.

E. *Respondent's satisfaction with the way earnings now compare.* After a respondent had indicated whether he or the comparison person was earning more, he was asked, "Which of these statements best shows how you feel about the way your earnings now compare to his earnings?" He was then handed a card which listed the following alternatives:

1. I am *very satisfied* with the way my earnings now compare to his earnings
2. I am *satisfied* with the way my earnings now compare to his earnings
3. I am *neither satisfied nor dissatisfied* with the way my earnings now compare to his earnings
4. I am *not too satisfied* with the way my earnings now compare to his earnings

5. I am *not at all satisfied* with the way my earnings compare
   to his earnings

For some analyses, each statement was assigned a score corresponding to the number on its left.

F. *Reasons for satisfaction or dissatisfaction with comparison.*
After R indicated his degree of satisfaction with the way earnings
compared, he was asked, "Could you tell me why you feel this
way?" The great majority of responses to this question were in
terms of comparison on dimensions other than pay (see Table 5).
These responses were coded in terms of the type of dimension
compared on, and whether R said he or the comparison person
stood higher on this non-pay dimension.

G. *Potential satisfaction with comparison.* Where R compared to someone making more than himself at present, but said
he was satisfied with the way earnings compared at present, he
was asked, "Thinking of what he is earning now, suppose you
never made as much as that—how would you feel?" Respondents
chose from a card one of the following five degrees of potential
satisfaction:

1. I would still feel very satisfied
2. I would feel satisfied
3. I would feel neither satisfied nor dissatisfied
4. I would feel not too satisfied
5. I would feel not at all satisfied

For some analyses, each statement was assigned a score corresponding to the number on its left.

Other measures available on each respondent included:

H. *Absolute pay rates.* These were available from company
records.

I. *Index of relative pay position.* Respondents reported their
age, education, length of service at the refinery, and the occupations of their brothers and brothers-in-law. On each of these
criteria, every respondent was coded as below the median on pay,
at the median, or above the median on pay for men like himself.
For example, the distribution on pay for men in each age cate-

gory was calculated so that every man in the category was assigned a score showing his relative position on pay for men of his
age.

In the same manner, each man was given a score showing his
pay position relative to men of his educational category; relative
to men of his seniority category; and to men of his family.

In addition to the scores showing each man's relative pay
position on each of these four dimensions, an over-all index of
relative pay position was constructed by adding each man's score
(corresponding to below, at, or above the median) on all four
dimensions.

J. *Perceived mobility chances.* These were measured by answers to the following checklist questions in the questionnaire:
"How good would you say your chances are of being promoted
one pay rate above your present rate?"

1. I'm *almost sure* to be advanced one pay rate
2. My chances are *good but it's not sure*
3. My chances are *about 50–50*
4. I have *some chance but it's not likely*
5. I have *almost no chance* of being advanced one pay rate
— I have no idea what my chances are

"Do you think you would ever be able to make more *outside*
Atlas than you're making here now?"

1. There's a good chance I could make more outside Atlas
2. Fair chance
4. Slight chance
5. Almost no chance
— I have no idea what my chances would be

K. *Actual mobility chances.* These are indicated by information obtained from each respondent regarding his position vis-à-
vis the company training program—especially whether he was
currently in such a program and, if not, whether he expected to
have the opportunity to enter the training program.

L. *Perception of personal responsibility.* This is indicated by answers to two questions asked in the interview. These questions and the alternative answers presented to respondents on printed cards are as follows: "For men who grew up when you did, how much would you say a man's chances for getting ahead in life depended on himself and how much on things beyond his control?"

1. *Almost entirely* on the man himself
2. *Mostly* on the man himself
3. *Somewhat* on the man himself
4. *Very little* on the man himself
5. *Not at all* on the man himself

"Thinking about Atlas, how much would you say advancement usually depends on how well a man can do a job and how much on other things?"

1. *Almost entirely* on how well a man can do a job
2. *Mostly* on how well a man can do a job
3. *Somewhat* on how well a man can do a job
4. *Very little* on how well a man can do a job
5. *Not at all* on how well a man can do a job

The numbers indicated above were assigned to alternative answers to these questions, in order to establish the correlation between answers to the questions. There was a moderate positive correlation between acceptance of responsibility, as measured by one question and as measured by the other ($r = +.29$). Moreover, each question, taken separately, was found to have a similar relation to the direction of comparisons chosen and to satisfaction with such comparisons. Therefore, since both questions appeared to be measuring a similar value dimension, an index of acceptance of personal responsibility was constructed simply by adding each respondent's scores on the two questions.

M. *Social definitions of wage position.* This is indicated by answers to the questionnaire item, "How often has anyone mentioned that a man like yourself deserves to be earning more money?"

The alternative responses provided in the questionnaire were:
1. It has happened *quite often*
2. It has happened *occasionally*
3. It has happened *once or twice*
4. It has *never* happened

CHAPTER 4

The Relation Between
Dissonance and Satisfaction

It has been maintained here that a man is much more likely to be satisfied with a comparison which is consonant than with one which is dissonant. We expect this to be true in two ways: first, that men are more likely to be dissatisfied with comparisons that have objective characteristics which would cause them to be accurately perceived as dissonant; and second, that men are more likely to be dissatisfied with comparisons which they perceive as dissonant. Hypotheses 1 and 2 express these expectations. We might expect the relation between satisfaction and *perceived* dissonance to be stronger than the relation between satisfaction and objective dissonance, since satisfaction is linked more directly to perception.

Although this discussion is concerned with satisfaction over specific wage *comparisons,* there is evidence that such satisfaction with comparisons is strongly related to general satisfaction with wages. Each respondent was asked on his questionnaire (reactions to comparisons were obtained as part of a prior interview)[1]

---

[1] Approximately an hour of time, and questions about a variety of other subjects, separated the questions about specific wage comparisons and the question on general feeling about earnings.

this question: "How well do you feel you've done up to now as far as earnings go?" Possible response categories were: very well; quite well; fairly well; not too well; not well at all.

The greater the satisfaction a man expressed with the specific comparisons he chose, the more content he was with his wages. At one extreme, among those who said they were "very satisfied" with both wage comparisons chosen, 90.2 per cent said they felt they had, in general, done "very well" or "quite well" with respect to their earnings. At the other extreme, among men who said they were "not too satisfied" or "not at all satisfied" with both specific wage comparisons, only 16.0 per cent said they had, in general, done "very well" or "quite well."

4.1. Objective Dissonance

We have postulated that comparisons to those earning more (upward comparisons) are most likely to be perceived as consonant when the comparer and comparison person are objectively similar in ways generally considered relevant to pay. We do not have data on all the objective similarities and differences between respondents and the comparison persons they chose. We do, however, have the following data which tell us something about the extent of objective similarity between the persons involved in any comparison.

1. *Occupational level of the comparison person.* It seems reasonable to assume that those comparison persons who are on a different occupational level than our respondents will differ from the respondent in a number of ways which are culturally considered relevant to pay. These differences include educational level, social class, style of life, and the kinds of skills involved in work. Comparison persons who are professional men are most likely to be different from blue-collar respondents in all of these ways, as well as in other ways. Men who are in white-collar occupations (clerical and sales) and men who are proprietors or managers of businesses are also likely to have backgrounds different

from our respondents, though not so different as that of professional persons.

2. *Place of work of the comparison person.* One similarity between men is the fact that they all work for the same company. Working under the same seniority system, getting companywide raises at the same time, being in physical contact, and merely having the same employer, establish a similarity among co-workers which is absent in comparisons among men who work for different employers. This certainly does not mean that co-workers are always more similar than outsiders. Similarities to outside men in education, age, type of work, school attended, etc., may be important, while co-workers can be different in important ways. However, the essential fact remains that working for the same company establishes some important similarities which should, in general, make co-workers be perceived as more similar than men outside the company.

3. *Family relations of the comparison person.* If the person chosen for comparison is a member of the respondent's immediate family, certain important similarities exist between the two persons. First, there is the fact of belonging to the same family. Also, there are almost certainly similarities in ethnic and religious background. There are, of course, important differences among family members (especially between in-law relations) which are pertinent to rate of pay. Age and education are probably the most important of these differences. But, in general, we may expect that respondents will perceive close relations (as defined in Chapter 3) as more similar to themselves than are non-relatives.

An important difference should be noted between the characteristic of occupational level and the characteristics of place of work and of family relationship. The occupational level of the comparison person is likely to be experienced by the comparer as *higher than, equal to, or lower than his own,* and to be associated with other characteristics, like education, which the comparer can easily see as superior, equal, or inferior to his own. However, the place of work and the family [1] of the comparison person appear likely to be seen by the comparer primarily as simply *similar to or different* from his own.

For example, when judging a wage comparison with someone earning more in terms of the occupational level of the two persons, the comparer is expected to say in effect: "This person is *superior* to me in occupational level and in the characteristics associated with occupational level; therefore (other things being equal) it is okay for his pay to be higher than mine." But when judging a wage comparison in terms of place of work or presence of a family relationship, the comparer is expected to say in effect: "This person is *different* in his place of work or in family and therefore it's more acceptable for him to earn more than me than it would be if he were someone at my own work place or someone in my own family." In each case, some degree of consonance is being established. But in one case the wage gap is seen as consonant with a superiority of the comparison person, while in the other case it is seen as consonant with a simple difference of the comparison person.

We expected, as stated in hypothesis 1A, that men who choose "upward" comparison persons who are similar in status will more often be dissatisfied with such comparisons than will men who choose persons of higher or simply different status. We will see next whether this expectation is correct when we consider separately similarities and differences in occupational level, in place of work, and in family.

Occupational Level. Table 1 shows how satisfied men are with upward comparisons, separately for comparisons to men at different occupational levels. Men who choose upward comparison persons who are professionals (i.e. most superior in general status) are most satisfied with those comparisons. Next highest in satis-

---

[1] This is especially likely to be true at the present site since many of the comparers do not know much about the family status of comparison persons.

faction with upward comparisons are men who choose "up" comparison persons in white-collar jobs (clerical, sales) or in managerial or proprietary jobs.

Men who choose for comparison those who are earning more than themselves, but who are also blue-collar workers, are least satisfied with the comparisons.

TABLE 1. SATISFACTION [a] WITH WAGE COMPARISONS TO THOSE EARNING MORE, SEPARATELY FOR COMPARISONS TO THOSE AT DIFFERENT OCCUPATIONAL LEVELS [b]

Occupational Level of Upward Comparison	Mean Satisfaction with Comparison	Number of Comparers [c]
Professional	2.23	(66)
Clerical or sales	2.33	(24)
Proprietor of own business; manager	2.42	(64)
Blue collar: foreman	2.59	(76)
Blue collar: skilled or semiskilled	2.63	(252)
Other (including farm and no mention)	2.43	(37)
Total	2.52	(519)

[a] Low scores indicate greater satisfaction with comparisons.
[b] Solid line joining two mean scores indicates that the difference is significant at the .01 level (1-tailed t test). Broken line joining two mean scores indicates that the difference is significant at the .10 level (1-tailed t test).
[c] For each comparer, a maximum of one comparison in each row is included in this table. However, a single comparer may have chosen two upward comparisons at different occupational levels, and so it is possible for the same comparer to be counted twice.

The data shown in Table 1 strongly support hypothesis 1. The more a comparison person who earns more than the comparer is similar to the comparer in occupational level (and thus, the more objectively dissonant the comparison), the less satisfied the comparer is.

Place of Work. Table 2 shows the relation of satisfaction with upward comparisons to the place of work of the comparison person.

Men who choose comparison persons who are earning more than themselves and who work for the same company are, on the average, less satisfied with such comparisons than are men who choose comparison persons who earn more in a *different* company.

Again, the prediction is supported: men who choose objectively dissonant comparisons are likely to be less satisfied with such comparisons.

Family Relationships. Table 3 shows satisfaction with comparisons to persons who earn more, separately for men who choose upward comparisons who are close relations and for men who chose upward comparisons who are non-relatives.

In general, men who choose upward comparisons who are relatives are more satisfied with the comparisons than are men who choose upward comparisons who are non-relatives. This finding is contrary to our prediction. Since we postulated that, in general, close relatives will be perceived as more similar than non-relatives, we expected that the fact of a close relative earning more than the respondent would usually be perceived as dissonant and thus unsatisfactory. How can we explain the contrary results?

TABLE 2. SATISFACTION [a] WITH WAGE COMPARISONS TO THOSE EARNING MORE, SEPARATELY FOR COMPARISONS WITHIN ATLAS AND OUTSIDE ATLAS [b, c]

Upward Comparison Person Works	Mean Satisfaction with Comparison	Number of Comparers
At Atlas	⌈2.60	(124)
Outside Atlas	⌊2.39	(203)

[a] Low scores indicate greater satisfaction with comparisons.
[b] For each comparer, a maximum of one comparison in each row is included in this table. Those men (122) who chose upward comparison persons whose place of work could not be identified are omitted from this table.
[c] A dashed line joining two mean scores indicates that the difference is significant at the .05 level (1-tailed *t* test).

One possible line of explanation is the possibility that, despite the similarities among close relatives, relatives are actually more dissimilar in important ways than are the non-relatives chosen.

TABLE 3. SATISFACTION [a] WITH WAGE COMPARISONS TO THOSE EARNING MORE, SEPARATELY FOR COMPARISONS TO CLOSE RELATIVES [b] AND TO NON-RELATIVES [c]

Upward Comparison Person Is	Mean Satisfaction with Comparison	Number of Comparers
A close relative	⌈2.26	(125)
Not a close relative	⌊2.62	(283)

[a] Low scores indicate greater satisfaction with comparisons.

[b] A close relative is defined as father, son, brother, mother, daughter, sister, and the in-law equivalents. Forty-seven men who gave no indication of whether the comparison person was a relative are not included in this table. For each comparer, a maximum of one comparison in each row is included in the table.

[c] A solid line joining two mean scores indicates that the difference is significant at the .001 level (2-tailed t test).

One important way in which relatives generally are unlike our respondents is that relatives more often work outside Atlas than do non-relatives. Could it be that the satisfaction expressed concerning comparisons to relatives who earn more results in part from the fact that relatives, more often than non-relatives chosen, work outside Atlas?

Table 4 shows satisfaction with upward comparisons to relatives and to non-relatives, holding place of work constant. It is apparent from this table that upward comparisons to relatives—within Atlas, at least—are still viewed as more satisfactory than are upward comparisons to non-relatives.

It may be, of course, that there are ways other than place of work in which upward comparison persons who are relatives tend to be more different from respondents than are non-relatives. However, the fact that the greatest number of relatives chosen for comparison are brothers or brothers-in-law, and therefore similar to respondents at least in age and sex, casts doubt on this explanation.

A second possible explanation is that our hypothesis stating that objective dissonance in comparisons will lead to dissatisfaction is basically incorrect. In the light of the data concerning satisfaction with comparisons at different occupational levels

TABLE 4. MEAN SATISFACTION [a] WITH UPWARD COMPARISONS, SEPARATELY FOR
COMPARISONS WHO WORK AT OR OUTSIDE ATLAS AND WHO
ARE CLOSE RELATIVES OR NON-RELATIVES [b, c]
(Number of Comparers in Parentheses)

Comparison Person Is	Comparison Person Works	
	At Atlas	Outside Atlas
Close relative	⌐2.05 (20)	2.37 (65)
Not close relative	⌐2.67 (92)	2.39 (111)

[a] Lower scores indicate greater satisfaction with comparisons.

[b] For any comparer, only the first upward comparison person who could be identified as a relative or non-relative and whose place of work was ascertainable is included in this table.

[c] Dashed line indicates that the difference between mean scores is significant at the .05 level (2-tailed *t* test).

(Table 1) and concerning satisfaction with comparisons inside and outside the company (Table 2), it would be hasty to accept this interpretation.

The most likely explanation of the result shown in Table 3 is a reluctance of the men interviewed to express (even to themselves) dissatisfaction over the fact of a close relative earning more than themselves. Exploratory interviews, as well as the later standardized interviews, often evoked sentiments condemning envy of those who are better off. Such sentiments were especially strong where relatives were concerned. Respondents were often quick to point out that they are not begrudging the fact that brothers or brothers-in-law are doing better than themselves. For example, one man whose brother-in-law is earning more than he, commented: "I don't feel I should begrudge him what he can get if he can make a go of it—it's up to him."

It is possible, therefore—though not provable from these data—that the dissonance produced by the fact of close relatives earning more actually does lead to feelings of discontent, but that these feelings are not always expressed. If this is true, then we need to amend hypothesis 1. We may still state that, in general, comparisons which are objectively dissonant will be perceived as such and experienced as unsatisfactory. However, in some instances where discontent is viewed as morally wrong, it appears that feelings of dissatisfaction will not be expressed (and/or perceptions of the objective situation will be distorted).

4.2. Perceived Consonance and Dissonance

We have predicted not only that objective dissonance will lead to feelings of dissatisfaction with comparisons, but that feelings of satisfaction or dissatisfaction will be subjectively based on perceptions of consonance or dissonance.

After each man expressed his degree of satisfaction with a specific wage comparison he was asked, "Could you tell me why you feel this way?" Table 5 shows the reasons given for feelings of satisfaction or dissatisfaction with comparisons to those who earn more than the respondent.

TABLE 5. REASONS GIVEN BY RESPONDENTS [a] FOR FEELING SATISFIED OR DISSATISFIED WITH SPECIFIC UPWARD WAGE COMPARISONS [b]
(Read Table Vertically)

Reasons Given for Feeling of Satisfaction or Dissatisfaction	Satisfaction with Upward Comparison		
	Satisfied (%)	Neither Satisfied nor Dissatisfied (%)	Dissatisfied (%)
Respondent has compensating advantages	44.6	19.5	0.0
Financial	16.1	5.4	0.0
Non-financial	28.5	14.1	0.0
Comparison person is superior	55.8	34.8	17.8
In what his job requires			
(education, skill, etc.)	44.6	22.8	13.7

TABLE 5.—Continued

Reasons Given for Feeling of Satisfaction or Dissatisfaction	Satisfaction with Upward Comparison		
	Satisfied %	Neither Satisfied nor Dis-satisfied %	Dissatisfied %
In seniority, experience, age	6.8	8.7	1.4
In personal qualities	4.4	3.3	2.7
Comparison person's job is different— unspecified	8.0	16.3	2.7
Respondent is equal or superior	1.2	9.8	75.4
In what his job requires (education, skill, etc.)	0.8	8.7	64.4
In seniority, experience, age	0.4	1.1	11.0
Respondent is not interested in comparing earnings	5.6	18.5	0.0
Respondent earns enough for his needs	2.8	4.4	0.0
Respondent wants more money, higher living standard	0.0	0.0	8.2
Other, or vague	3.6	10.9	16.4
Number of comparers	(249)	(92)	(73)

[a] The percentages of reasons in each column add up to more than 100, since a maximum of two reasons was coded for each respondent.

[b] The reasons given by each man for his feelings about a maximum of one comparison are included in any single column.

Reasons for Feeling Satisfied. Of those who said they are satisfied with comparisons to men who earn more, over half (56 per cent) mentioned ways in which comparison persons are superior to themselves, as justifying the difference in wages. More education, more seniority, being older, having more skills, having more responsibility, and having worked harder for advancement are among the superiorities of the comparison person mentioned.

A large proportion (45 per cent) of those who expressed satisfaction with upward comparisons explained their feelings by pointing to compensating advantages which they enjoy. Such items as having a better benefit program at Atlas, working more steadily, liking their own work better, and having a cleaner job are typical of the compensating advantages mentioned.

About 8 per cent of those satisfied emphasized the difference in jobs per se, without specifying which man deserves more pay. These men mentioned the fact of working for different companies, different departments, or different industries, implying that these essential differences explain the difference in wages. About 6 per cent of those satisfied said they were not interested in comparing wages; 1 per cent mentioned ways in which they are equal or superior to the men who earn more; and 4 per cent gave other reasons.

These data show that an overwhelming majority of men explain their satisfaction with upward comparisons in terms of differences between themselves and the comparison person on dimensions related directly or indirectly to pay. These differences are usually either some superiority of the comparison person or some compensating advantage enjoyed by the respondent. In either case, what these men seem to be saying, in effect, is: "I am satisfied to be earning less, because there is some other difference between us which makes the wage difference okay." Or, in our theoretical terms, "I am satisfied because the difference in wages is consonant with other differences between us."

It is noteworthy that so few respondents (about 3 per cent) answered merely in terms of the wage difference—saying they earned enough for their needs—without relating the wage difference to some other relevant differences between the individuals.

Reasons for Dissatisfaction. Among those who are dissatisfied with earning less than the comparison persons, a large majority (75 per cent) justify their feelings in terms of their own equality or superiority in ways directly relevant to pay. Mention of the respondent's high level of education, skill, responsibility, seniority, and experience and/or the comparison person's low standing in these respects are typical of the kinds of reasons included in this category.

Again, very few men explained their dissatisfaction merely in terms of the money difference or in the closely related terms of their wish for more material things. Only 8 per cent mentioned these reasons, and among these men, many gave additional answers in terms of the relative standing of comparer and comparison person on attributes other than earnings.

Eighteen per cent of those dissatisfied mention some *superiority* of the comparison person—most often in an attempt to give both sides of the issue. Three per cent mention the differences per se in occupation, industry, etc.

There also were a relatively large number of answers (16.4 per cent) made by dissatisfied men which do not fit in the categories mentioned. Detailed examination of these uncategorized answers reveals that many are vague and non-specific—sometimes a mere restatement of dissatisfaction.

The data for dissatisfied men thus also support hypothesis 2. The great majority of men explain their feelings of dissatisfaction in terms of dissonance between differences in pay and differences on attributes related to pay.

Reasons for Feeling "Neutral" about Comparison. The reasons given by those who say they are "neither satisfied nor dissatisfied" with upward comparisons indicate that their "neutrality" of feeling is based on cross-pressures exerted by perceptions of consonance and perceptions of dissonance. About one-third of these men mention some way in which the *comparison person* is superior, but 10 per cent mention some way in which *they* themselves are equal or superior.

The most striking difference shown by this group is the relatively large proportion (19 per cent) who say they are not interested in comparing earnings. There appears to be a tendency in this group to avoid thinking about comparisons and to shut off their feelings about comparisons ("neither satisfied nor dissatisfied") when they are forced to compare.

Reasons Given for Satisfaction with Downward Comparisons.
The data concerning reasons given for feeling satisfied or dissatisfied with comparisons to those who earn less (these data are not shown here) also support hypothesis 2. As expected, almost all men who compared themselves to those persons who earn less than themselves expressed satisfaction with the comparisons. The question, "Why?" evoked only a restatement of the fact of earning more by about one-third of these men. However, over one-third mentioned their superiority on some attribute (education, experience, etc.) related to pay and evidently justifying their higher pay. About 10 per cent mentioned some way in which the comparison person was equal or superior, thus emphasizing their own good fortune in earning more.

Of the handful of men (12) who expressed dissatisfaction with comparisons to those earning less than themselves, half mentioned some equality or superiority of the comparison person, evidently as a protest over the injustice done to the other person.

4.3. Summary

The data presented here have offered some support for hypothesis 1—that objectively dissonant comparisons will be judged as unsatisfactory. Men choosing comparison persons who earn more but who are at a higher occupational level or work for a different employer were more likely to be satisfied with comparisons than were those choosing upward comparisons who are similar to themselves in these ways.

However, the finding that men are more satisfied with upward comparisons to relatives than they are with upward comparisons to non-relatives goes contrary to hypothesis 1. We suggested the explanation that, for moral reasons, men are reluctant to express the dissatisfaction they feel concerning certain comparisons.

The data offer strong support for hypothesis 2—that men who are satisfied with specific comparisons subjectively base their feelings on a consonance between the wage difference and other related differences between the men; and that men who are dissatisfied with comparisons explain their feelings in terms of a dissonance between the wage difference and other related differences. Some of the concrete kinds of reasons offered by individuals for feelings of satisfaction or dissatisfaction with wage comparisons were mentioned.

CHAPTER 5

Relative Pay and Absolute Pay

We have predicted, in hypothesis 3, that men who earn less than others like themselves will more often choose dissonant comparisons. We expect also that men who are doing poorly on pay, compared to those like themselves in age, seniority, education, and family, will more often be dissatisfied with the wage comparisons they make. These relationships have been predicted to hold true regardless of absolute pay rate.

5.1. Direction of Comparisons

Let us look first to see whether relative pay position [1] makes a difference in whether or not a man chooses comparison persons who are earning more or earning less than himself. Table 6 shows that men who are doing poorly on pay, relative to those like themselves, are much more likely than others to choose comparison persons who are above them in pay. As relative pay position goes up, there is a sharp reduction in the proportion of men who compare themselves only to those above them, and a large increase in

---

[1] See Chapter 3 for a description of the construction of the relative pay position index.

the proportion of men choosing comparison persons below them in pay. This result supports the prediction of hypothesis 3A.

TABLE 6. DIRECTION OF COMPARISONS CHOSEN BY MEN AT
DIFFERENT RELATIVE PAY POSITIONS [a,b]

Relative Pay Position	Chooses Comparisons Who Earn			Total (%)	Number of Men
	More Only (%)	Both More and Less (%)	Less Only (%)		
Low	⌈52.0	38.7	9.3⌉	100	(204)
Medium	⌊34.3	45.7	20.0⌐	100	(105)
High	⌊17.0	50.9	32.1⌋	100	(165)
Total	35.9	44.5	19.6	100	(474)

[a] Fifteen men who did not choose two comparisons are omitted from this table.
[b] Solid line joining two percentages indicates a difference significant beyond the .01 level (1-tailed test of percentage difference).

The question immediately arises as to whether or not the relation between *relative* pay and direction of comparisons chosen is independent of *absolute* pay rate. That is, does a poor relative pay position lead to more "up" comparisons regardless of the actual amount a man is earning?

To answer this question, a partial correlation analysis was performed. For this analysis, successive differences between nine standard company pay rates were counted as equal units. (Actual money differences between successive rates are approximately equal.) The relative pay index, with nine possible positions, was treated as an equal interval scale,[2] and the number of upward comparisons was treated as a three-point scale—the points being (1) no upward comparisons, (2) one upward comparison, and (3) two upward comparisons made by each man.

The partial correlation between *relative* pay position and

---

[2] The relative pay index only approximates an equal interval scale. The partial correlation coefficients between this scale and other variables should, therefore, be considered to be an approximation of the true relationships among these variables.

number of upward comparisons chosen, with *absolute* pay rate held constant, is −.21 (significant at beyond the .01 level in a 2-tailed test). That is, as a man does better on pay relative to those like himself, he makes fewer upward comparisons.

The partial correlation between *absolute* pay rate and direction of comparison, when differences in *relative* pay position are held constant, is −.04, a small and non-significant relation. A man's absolute pay level, in itself, makes little difference, then, in whether he compares up or down. It is his relative pay position that matters most.

The relation between relative position and direction of comparison holds when controlled by other important factors in the situation. Men who stand low on relative pay position choose more upward comparisons regardless of (1) feelings of personal responsibility, (2) social definitions of their position, (3) whether they believe they could ever earn more outside, and (4) whether or not they are in the company training program. The tendency to choose upward is especially marked, however, for men who are not now in the training program and who do not expect to be.

5.2. Status of Upward Comparisons Chosen

Men who are doing poorly relative to others like themselves are likely to compare themselves to those who are earning more than themselves. But what kind of people are the upward comparison persons who are chosen?

According to hypothesis 3B, men at a low relative pay position, when they compare themselves to those who earn more than themselves, are likely to choose persons of similar status—specifically those of the same occupational level and those who work at the same company.[3]

---

[3] The data shown in Table 3 indicate that the similarity of comparison persons as being close relatives or non-relatives involves special problems of interpretation and has a meaning to respondents which is different from similarity of comparison persons in occupational level or in place of work. The status of comparison persons as relatives or non-relatives is, therefore, not considered when examining the status of comparison persons.

TABLE 7. OCCUPATIONAL LEVEL OF UPWARD COMPARISON PERSONS,[a]
SEPARATELY FOR COMPARISONS CHOSEN BY MEN AT
DIFFERENT RELATIVE PAY POSITIONS [b]

Choose Upward Comparisons Who Are	Relative Pay Position		
	Below Median %	Near Median %	Above Median %
Professionals	10.3	13.1	20.0
Clerical, sales	2.2	6.0	5.2
Proprietors, managers	10.3	15.5	14.8
Blue-collar: foremen	12.0	10.7	14.8
Blue-collar: skilled, semi-skilled	56.0	48.8	39.1
Other (farm; blue collar, unspecified; etc.)	9.2	6.0	6.1
Total per cent	100.0	100.0	100.0
Total number of comparers	(183)	(86)	(119)

[a] Only the first upward comparison chosen by any respondent is included in this table.
[b] Dashed line indicates that the percentage difference is significant at the .05 level (1-tailed test). Solid line joining two percentages indicates that the difference is significant at the .01 level or beyond (1-tailed test of percentage difference).

Occupational Level of Comparison Persons. Table 7 shows the occupational level of upward comparison persons, separately for comparisons chosen by men at different relative pay positions.[4] The data show that those who stand relatively low on pay chose upward comparisons at their own occupational level (blue-collar, skilled or semi-skilled) significantly more often than did men who are relatively high on pay. Those whose relative pay position is near the median chose an intermediate number of upward comparisons at their own occupational level.

Men who are relatively low on pay chose professional persons as upward comparisons significantly less often than did men who are high on pay. The "lows" also chose upward comparisons who are in white-collar occupations (clerical or sales) somewhat less

---

[4] The assumption is made here that the comparison persons chosen spontaneously by respondents (i.e., the most salient comparisons) are those which are in some way important to the respondents. One justification for this assumption lies in the meaningfulness of the results obtained wtih the present research technique.

often, and chose proprietors and managers slightly less often than did men whose relative pay position is near or above the median.

These data support hypothesis 3B. The lower their relative pay position, the more likely are men to choose upward comparison persons of similar occupational status. And, thus, the lower the relative position, the more dissonant the comparison.

The relationship between relative pay position and the occupational level of upward comparison persons is maintained when controlled (1) by whether men believe they could earn more outside Atlas, (2) by social definitions of wage position, and (3) by position vis-a-vis the company training program. The relation between low relative position and choice of dissonant comparisons also persists regardless of how much personal responsibility is accepted, but is strongest among men who accept least responsibility for their own fate. This latter tendency is consistent with the results of Table 8 and is in accord with our expectation that men who reject personal responsibility for their fate are likely to choose dissonant comparisons.

Place of Work of Comparison Persons. Among men who are relatively low on pay and who chose comparison persons earning more than themselves, 41 per cent chose persons at Atlas. Among men whose relative pay position is near or above the median, 36 per cent chose upward comparisons at the same company. Although this difference is small and statistically non-significant, it is in the direction predicted. That is, from the standpoint of where upward comparison persons work, men relatively low on pay chose objectively dissonant comparisons somewhat more often than did others.

5.3. Satisfaction with Upward Comparisons

We have seen that men who stand low on relative pay position are more likely to choose upward comparisons of similar status—particularly in occupational status. Such comparisons are, according to our thinking, objectively dissonant. We would expect, therefore, as stated in hypothesis 3C, that men low on relative pay position are most likely to be dissatisfied with upward comparisons.

TABLE 8. MEAN SCORES OF PRESENT SATISFACTION [a] WITH UPWARD
COMPARISONS, SEPARATELY FOR MEN OF DIFFERENT
RELATIVE PAY POSITIONS AND DIFFERENT DEGREES
OF ACCEPTANCE OF RESPONSIBILITY [b,c]
(Number of Comparers in Parentheses)

Relative Pay Position	Acceptance of Responsibility			Total
	Little	Moderate	Great	
Low	3.02 (64)	2.60 (68)	2.38 (52)	2.68 (184)
Medium	2.43 (41)	2.20 (27)	2.21 (17)	2.31 (85)
High	2.28 (44)	2.12 (33)	2.22 (37)	2.21 (114)
Total	2.64 (149)	2.39 (128)	2.30 (106)	2.46 (383)

[a] Lower score indicates greater satisfaction.
[b] Three men who did not answer both questions comprising the acceptance of responsibility index are not included in this table.
[c] Solid line joining two mean scores indicates that the difference is significant at the .01 level or beyond (1-tailed t test). Dashed line joining two mean scores indicates significant difference at the .05 level or beyond (1-tailed t test).

Table 8 shows mean scores of satisfaction with upward comparisons, separately for men at different relative pay positions. The data show that as relative pay position increases, satisfaction with upward comparisons increases too. (Although satisfaction rises progressively with relative pay position, the statistically significant differences in satisfaction are between those low in relative position and those either medium or high.) Thus, we see that, in general, low relative pay position leads not only to the choice of more upward comparisons, but also to greater dissatisfaction with the upward comparisons made. However, this is not always the case. Table 8 shows also the relation between relative pay position and satisfaction with upward comparisons separately for men who differ in how much they accept personal responsibility for their occupational fate.

The data show that as feelings of personal responsibility increase, relative pay position has less effect on satisfaction with comparisons. Among those who accept little responsibility for their fate, relative pay position has a highly significant effect on satisfaction with upward comparisons. Among men who accept moderate personal responsibility, relative position exerts a lesser but still significant effect on satisfaction. But among men who accept great personal responsibility for their fate, relative pay position has little effect on satisfaction with comparisons.

It is striking to recall that men who are low in relative pay position choose upward comparisons more often than others, regardless of how much personal responsibility they accept. However, once having chosen upward comparisons, those who also accept great personal responsibility are more likely to express satisfaction with the comparisons than are those who reject responsibility.

It appears probable that men who stand relatively low on pay do not feel justified in expressing dissatisfaction if they believe that their low position is their own fault. Moreover, for men who accept personal responsibility for their fate, dissatisfaction may be equivalent to feelings of personal failure. Such men would tend to avoid these painful feelings of failure by thinking of some justification of why their wages are lower than those of comparison persons.

Relative Pay, Absolute Pay, and Satisfaction. When one considers the relationship between relative pay position and satisfaction with comparisons, the question arises again as to whether the relationship shown holds true when we keep absolute pay rate constant. A further question of interest is whether absolute pay position or relative pay position has the greater effect on satisfaction with upward comparisons.

To answer these questions, a second partial correlation analysis was performed. The same relative pay position and actual pay-rate scales described above were used for this analysis. Satisfaction with upward comparisons was represented by a nine-point scale, constructed by assigning values of 1 through 5 to the various degrees of satisfaction with each comparison and combining the data for the two possible upward comparisons made by each respondent.

When absolute pay rate is held constant, the correlation between relative pay position and satisfaction with upward comparisons is +.14. As relative pay position goes higher, satisfaction with upward comparisons increases too. Although this relationship is not strong, it is significant in our large sample at the .01 level (using a 2-tailed test).

When, however, we hold relative pay position constant, the correlation between absolute pay rate and satisfaction with upward comparisons is +.01, clearly non-significant. In other words, actual pay rate, by itself, has no effect on satisfaction with comparisons.

The necessarily high correlation between actual pay rate and relative pay position which exists in our population, as well as elsewhere, means that a higher absolute pay rate will usually be indirectly associated with greater satisfaction concerning comparisons. Our results show clearly, however, that it is relative position, and not absolute pay level, which exerts the important influence on satisfaction.

5.4. Summary

The data presented in this chapter provide some support for the hypothesis that men who stand low in relative pay position are more likely to choose objectively dissonant wage comparisons. We saw this to be true in two ways. First, men who are low in relative position are more likely to choose comparison persons who earn more than themselves. Second, when choosing such "up" comparisons, they are more likely to choose comparisons whose status is similar to their own.

The results give support also to our expectation that men standing relatively low in pay will be less satisfied than others with the comparisons they choose. We saw, however, that this is true only when those who are doing relatively poorly accept little responsibility for their position.

Finally, the data of this chapter show that the influence of *relative* pay position on types of comparisons chosen, and on satisfaction with comparisons, is more important than the influence of *absolute* pay position.

CHAPTER 6

Mobility Chances

6.1. Mobility Chances Inside the Company

Differences Among Measures of Mobility Chances. Hypothesis 5 states that "men who have good chances for upward mobility will be more likely than others to make potentially dissonant wage comparisons."

In stating this hypothesis, we did not differentiate between mobility chances *inside* the company and mobility chances *outside* it. The data show this distinction to be an important one. Therefore, mobility chances outside Atlas will be discussed separately—in the next section of this chapter. In the present section, we will consider only mobility chances within Atlas.

In considering mobility chances within Atlas, we need to make a further distinction—that between objective and perceived chances.

Although we predicted that both objective and perceived mobility chances would have an important effect on wage comparisons, our principal measure of *perceived* chances ("How good would you say your chances are of being promoted one pay rate above your present rate?") had much less influence on choice of wage comparisons than did *objective* mobility chances.

Whether this signifies that perception actually was less important in this situation, or that our measure of perceived mobility chances was inadequate, is not clear. In any case, we will consider in this chapter principally the effects of objective mobility chances.

Objective Mobility Chances. The measure of a man's objective mobility chances used here is his position with regard to the company training program. Four principal categories can be distinguished: [1]

1. Men now in the training program,
2. Men who finished the training program,
3. Men who haven't had the opportunity to enter—but think they probably *will* have a chance to enter in the future ("Temporarily Barred" group),
4. Men who haven't had the opportunity to enter—and think they probably *won't* have a chance to enter in the future ("Permanently Barred" group).

(It will be noted that these classifications are not entirely based on objective position. Groups 3 and 4 are both in the objective position of not having had an opportunity to enter the program, but differ in their perceptions of future opportunities.)

In testing hypotheses 5 and 6, we will first present our results, without attempting to interpret fully each specific datum. The pattern of these results will then be discussed, in an attempt to interpret their significance.

Direction of Comparisons. We predicted (in hypothesis 5A) that men with good mobility chances will more often choose comparison persons who earn more than themselves. Table 9 shows that just the reverse occurs. Only one-fifth of men in the training

---

[1] Men who dropped out of the program (15), who decided not to enter (44), who didn't know whether they would have an opportunity to enter (22), or who did not give complete information about their position vis-à-vis the program (11), are not included in this analysis.

program chose only "up" comparisons. But significantly larger proportions—46 per cent and 42 per cent—of men in groups outside the training program chose only "up" comparisons. Men who have finished the training program were intermediate—choosing only "up" comparisons in 32 per cent of the cases.

TABLE 9. DIRECTION OF COMPARISONS CHOSEN, SEPARATELY FOR MEN IN DIFFERENT POSITIONS VIS-À-VIS COMPANY TRAINING PROGRAM [a, b]

Training Program Position	Choose Comparison Persons Who Earn			Total (%)	Number of Comparers
	More Only (%)	Both More and Less (%)	Less Only (%)		
In program now	20.7	57.1	22.1	100.0	(140)
Finished program	32.1	47.2	20.7	100.0	(53)
Temporarily barred ..	46.0	35.1	18.9	100.0	(74)
Permanently barred ..	41.6	38.1	20.3	100.0	(118)

[a] Men who decided not to enter the program (44) ; who dropped out (15) ; who did not have an opportunity to enter, but "don't know" about future prospects (22) ; who gave incomplete information about their training position (11) ; or who did not choose two comparisons (12) are not included in this table.
[b] Solid line joining two percentages indicates a significant difference at the .01 level or beyond (2-tailed test of percentage difference).

Men outside the training program choose "upward" more often than those inside the program even when we take into account differences in pay rate; in social influences to earn more; in acceptance of personal responsibility; and in perception of chances to earn more outside Atlas. However, differences in relative pay position have an important effect on the general disposition of those outside the training program to compare upward. (See Table 10.)

TABLE 10. PERCENTAGES OF MEN WHO CHOOSE ONLY UPWARD COMPARISONS,
SEPARATELY FOR MEN IN DIFFERENT POSITIONS VIS-À-VIS TRAINING
PROGRAM AND IN DIFFERENT RELATIVE PAY POSITIONS [a, b]
(Number of Comparers in Parentheses)

Training Program Position	Relative Pay Position		
	Low (%)	Medium (%)	High (%)
In program now	⌐32.1 (53)	⌐17.0 (47)	⌐10.0 (40)
Finished program	50.0 (6)	45.5 (11)	25.0 (36)
Temporarily barred	∟57.9 (38)	33.3 (15)	∟33.3 (21)
Permanently barred	∟63.2 (57)	∟52.9 (17)	9.1 (44)

[a] Only men who chose two comparisons are included in this table.
[b] Solid line joining two percentages indicates a significant difference, at the .01 level (2-tailed test of percentage difference). Dashed line joining two percentages indicates a significant difference, at the .05 level (2-tailed test).

The data show that men who are permanently barred from the training program (and the quick mobility chances it offers) are significantly more likely than those in the program to choose upward comparisons—but only when the permanently barred men are doing relatively poorly or are merely average on pay. Those who are permanently barred from the training program, but who are already doing relatively well on wages, actually compare upward somewhat *less* often than those in the program. However, those who are temporarily barred from the program choose upward comparisons more often than those in the program, regardless of their relative pay position.

Status of Comparison Persons. We have predicted (hypothesis 5B) that highly mobile men, when they choose comparison persons earning more than themselves, will choose persons who

are now or are potentially similar to themselves (i.e., dissonant
or potentially dissonant comparisons). We expected, on the other
hand, that "low mobile" men, when they make upward comparisons, will choose men who are dissimilar to themselves (i.e., consonant comparisons). Let us see how these predictions turned out.

Occupational level of comparisons: Table 11 shows that
among men who have finished the training program, a strikingly

TABLE 11. OCCUPATIONAL LEVEL OF UPWARD COMPARISONS,[a] SEPARATELY FOR
PERSONS CHOSEN BY MEN IN DIFFERENT POSITIONS
VIS-À-VIS COMPANY TRAINING PROGRAM [b]

Choose Upward Comparisons Who Are	Training Program Position			
	In Now (%)	Finished (%)	Temporarily Barred (%)	Permanently Barred (%)
Professionals	18.2	32.6	9.8	5.2
Clerical, sales	0.9	7.0	6.6	4.2
Proprietors, managers	12.7	25.6	8.2	10.4
Blue-collar: foremen	11.8	9.3	13.1	13.5
Blue-collar: skilled or semi-skilled	50.0	18.6	45.9	60.4
Other (farm; blue-collar, unspecified; etc.)	6.4	7.0	16.4	6.3
Total	100.0	100.0	100.0	100.0
Number of comparers	(110)	(43)	(61)	(96)

[a] Only the first upward comparison chosen by any respondent is included in this table.
[b] Dashed line joining two percentages indicates a significant difference at the .05 level
(2-tailed test of percentage difference). Solid line joining two percentages indicates a
significant difference at the .01 level (2-tailed test of percentage difference).

large proportion—over half—choose upward comparisons who
are on a higher occupational level. Such comparisons are, by our
definition, consonant.

Contrary to our expectation, those in the training program were more likely to choose upward comparisons of a higher occupational level than were men outside the training program— although not nearly as likely as men who had finished the program. That is to say, the upward comparisons chosen by men in the program were more consonant than upward comparisons chosen by those outside the program.

Place of work of comparison persons: In addition to more often choosing upward comparisons on the same occupational level, men who are permanently barred from the training program more often chose upward comparisons within the same company. Table 12 shows that when "permanently barred" men compared

TABLE 12. PLACE OF WORK OF UPWARD COMPARISON PERSONS,
SEPARATELY FOR PERSONS CHOSEN BY MEN IN
DIFFERENT POSITIONS VIS-À-VIS
TRAINING PROGRAM [a,b]

Training Program Position	Choose Upward Comparison Persons Who Work		Total (%)	Number of Comparers
	At Atlas (%)	Outside Atlas (%)		
In now	⌈34.9⌉	65.1	100.0	(83)
Finished	19.4	80.6	100.0	(36)
Temporarily barred	24.5	75.5	100.0	(49)
Permanently barred	⌊48.0⌋	52.0	100.0	(77)

[a] For each respondent, only the first upward comparison person whose place of work was identified is included in this table. Ninety-four respondents who gave no indication of whether the comparison persons chosen work at Atlas are not included in this table.
[b] Solid line joining two percentages indicates that the difference is significant at the .01 level (2-tailed test of percentage difference); dashed line indicates difference is significant at the .05 level or beyond; broken line indicates difference is significant at the .10 level or beyond.

themselves to persons earning more than themselves, 48 per cent chose comparison persons at Atlas. This contrasts to 35 per cent of those in the training program and 19 per cent of men who completed the program who chose upward comparisons within their own company. Men who are temporarily barred from the training program again chose more consonant upward comparisons than the permanently barred group, choosing upward comparisons at their own company in only 25 per cent of the cases.

(The greater likelihood of those permanently barred from the program choosing upward comparisons at Atlas tends to hold true when other important variables—relative pay position, chances to earn more outside, social pressures, and acceptance of responsibility—are taken into account.)

The data concerning the occupational level of comparison persons and the place of work of comparison persons are, thus, contrary to hypothesis 5B. Men with the poorest mobility chances (those permanently barred from training) are more likely than those with the best mobility chances (those in the training program) to choose dissonant comparisons. Men who have been temporarily barred from the program stand intermediate between these two groups.

Present Satisfaction with Upward Comparisons. We expected to find differences between highly mobile and non-mobile men in their satisfaction with comparisons to those who earn more. Although hypothesis 6 concerns differences in *potential* satisfaction, let us first look at *present* satisfaction with upward comparisons. (We stated no hypothesis concerning the effect of mobility chances on *present* satisfaction with comparisons.) Table 13 shows that men who have been barred from the training program are somewhat less satisfied presently with upward comparisons than are the highly mobile men within the training program. Although the difference is small, the greater dissatisfaction of men outside the program parallels the fact that such men, when comparing upward, are more likely to choose dissonant comparisons (men of similar status). Men who have finished the training program are most satisfied with upward comparisons—significantly more so than those who never had an opportunity to enter the program. The high satisfaction of those who finished the pro-

TABLE 13. MEAN SCORES OF PRESENT SATISFACTION [a] WITH UPWARD
COMPARISONS, SEPARATELY FOR MEN IN DIFFERENT
POSITIONS VIS-À-VIS TRAINING PROGRAM [b, c]

Training Program Position	Mean Satis- faction Score	Number of Com- parers
In program now	2.40	(110)
Finished program	⌈2.26	(43)
Temporarily barred	⌊2.57	(60)
Permantly barred	2.55	(96)

[a] Lower numbers indicate greater satisfaction with upward comparisons.
[b] Eighty-eight men who did not choose any upward comparisons, or who did not indicate their degree of satisfaction with the comparison, are not included in this table.
[c] Broken line indicates difference between mean scores is significant at the .10 level (2-tailed *t* test).

gram parallels their choice of consonant upward comparisons—especially their frequent choice of men at higher occupational levels.

Potential Satisfaction with Upward Comparisons. Besides knowing how satisfied men are at present with upward wage comparisons, we wish to know also how satisfied they are with the prospect of remaining below the comparison persons in the future. Table 14 shows that, among those presently satisfied with comparisons, men with the best mobility chances (those in the training program) express the greatest dissatisfaction with the possibility of *remaining* below comparison persons in wages. Those who have already risen on the mobility ladder (men who have finished the training program) and men who expect to have a chance to enter the program are intermediate in potential dissatisfaction; while men with the poorest mobility situation (those permanently barred from the program) expressed least dissatisfaction with the prospect of remaining lower on wages.

Table 14 also shows that the relation between training-pro-

TABLE 14. MEAN SATISFACTION [a] WITH THE PROSPECT OF REMAINING
BELOW UPWARD COMPARISON PERSONS, SEPARATELY FOR MEN IN
DIFFERENT POSITIONS VIS-À-VIS TRAINING PROGRAM
AND IN DIFFERENT RELATIVE PAY POSITIONS [b,c]
(Number of Comparers in Parentheses)

Training Program Position	Relative Pay Position			Total
	Below Median	Near Median	Above Median	
In program now	3.08 (39)	⌜2.92 (33)	⌜2.98 (25)	⌜3.00 (97)
Finished program	2.90 (5)	∟2.25 (10)	2.92 (25)	2.75 (40)
Temporarily barred	2.92 (25)	2.50 (11)	2.50 (14)	2.71 (50)
Permanently barred	2.95 (44)	2.58 (13)	∟2.11 (22)	∟2.38 (79)

[a] Low numbers indicate greater satisfaction at prospect of remaining below those who earn more.
[b] Only men who indicated *present* satisfaction with an upward comparison were asked about their *potential* satisfaction.
[c] Solid line between two means indicates the difference is significant at the .01 (1-tailed *t* test). Broken line between two means indicates the difference is significant at the .10 level (1-tailed *t* test).

gram position and potential satisfaction is conditioned by relative pay position. Men who are permanently barred from the training program are significantly more satisfied than others with the prospect of remaining lower than comparison persons only when their wages are already relatively high. Men who are now in the training program are dissatisfied with the prospect of remaining lower than comparisons regardless of their present relative wage position.

These results showing the relation between within-company mobility chances, on the one hand, and potential satisfaction with comparisons on the other, support hypothesis 6. They are, moreover, a reversal of the findings concerning present satisfaction. Whereas highly mobile men (now in training) were moderate in satisfaction with being presently in a lower position, their feelings concerning *remaining* lower are different, making them the most potentially dissatisfied group.

We have seen that men in the training program, when choosing upward, chose only a moderate proportion of dissonant comparisons (i.e., a moderate number of those similar in occupational status and place of work). Although this fact corresponds to the moderate present satisfaction of the in-training group, it does not explain their great potential dissatisfaction. Is their potential dissatisfaction related to some difference in the kind of upward comparison persons they choose? Or does their expectation of advancement lead to potential dissatisfaction, without altering the kinds of comparisons made?

To throw light on this question, let us consider those men who said they are presently satisfied with earning less than a comparison person. Before any question was asked concerning the prospect of *remaining* lower, each man was asked, concerning his present (satisfied) feelings: "Could you tell me why you feel this way?"

Hypothesis 5C states that highly mobile men, when they are presently satisfied with an upward comparison, will more often than others give as a reason their inferior standing on a dimension on which their position will improve.

Although reasons given for being presently satisfied with earning less were not coded specifically to test this particular prediction, the data offer support for the prediction. Among highly mobile men (in training) who are satisfied with presently earning less than comparison persons, 12 per cent mentioned differences in seniority, experience, or age (dimensions on which their position will change) as a reason for their present satisfaction. This compares to 6 per cent who give such reasons among the Temporarily Barred and only 1 per cent among the Permanently Barred. (The difference between those Permanently Barred and those In-Training is statistically significant.)

Even clearer support for the hypothesis is obtained when we

examine answers given by those who are presently satisfied with upward comparisons to the question, "How does it happen that you are now earning less than he?"

Table 15 shows that, again in answer to this question, highly

TABLE 15. REASONS [a] GIVEN FOR EARNING LESS THAN UPWARD
COMPARISONS BY MEN WHO ARE PRESENTLY SATISFIED
WITH SUCH COMPARISONS, SEPARATELY FOR MEN
AT DIFFERENT POSITIONS VIS-À-VIS THE
COMPANY TRAINING PROGRAM [b]

Reasons Given as Justification for Earning Less	Training	Program	Position
	In Now (%)	Tempo- arily Barred (%)	Perma- nently Barred (%)
Education, training, special skills	24.4	33.3	21.3
Special demands of job	8.9	16.7	20.0
Seniority, experience, age	18.9	8.3	2.5
Personal qualities	3.3	6.3	1.3
Jobs are different	27.8	18.8	23.8
Comparison person works more hours	3.3	6.3	5.0
Luck	5.6	2.1	13.8
Physical handicaps	0.0	2.1	3.8
Other	5.6	4.2	7.5
No answer	2.2	2.1	1.3
Number of men presently satisfied with upward comparisons	(90)	(48)	(80)

[a] The percentage in each column may exceed 100 per cent, since a respondent could give more than one reason.
For each respondent, only reasons given concerning the first upward comparison with which he is presently satisfied, are included.
[b] Solid line joining two percentages indicates the difference is significant at the .01 level (1-tailed test). Dashed line joining two percentages indicates the difference is significant at the .05 level (1-tailed test for "seniority"; 2-tailed test for other dashed lines).

mobile men (in training) mention significantly more often than others greater seniority, experience, or age as explaining the present difference in earnings. Since the comparers will attain greater seniority, experience, and age as time goes by, it is obvious that such reasons will not suffice to justify their continuing to earn less than the comparison person is earning now. The data suggest, therefore, that highly mobile persons either purposely choose those comparisons which are most potentially dissonant, or else focus more on whatever potential dissonance does exist between themselves and the comparison persons who are chosen for other reasons.

Other noteworthy differences among men who are presently satisfied with upward comparisons but are in different positions vis-à-vis the training program are that (1) men who are permanently barred from the program are significantly more likely than others to attribute the higher standing of comparison persons to past luck; and (2) those who in the Permanently Barred group are significantly more likely than those now in the training program to mention special demands of the job (heavy work, dirty work, etc.) as explanations for present wage differences. The characteristics stressed more by those permanently barred from the training program—special job features and past luck—are not so likely to be changed by time as are the attributes of seniority, experience, and age.

Discussion. The data of this section give some support to hypothesis 5—that men with good mobility chances will more often choose *potentially* dissonant comparisons and that they will more often be *potentially* dissatisfied with the comparisons they choose. Specifically, our results have supported the predictions that (1) highly mobile men will more often give as reasons for present satisfaction their inferior standing on a dimension on which their position will improve; and (2) highly mobile men will more often express dissatisfaction with the prospect of remaining below comparison persons in the future.

However, the data do not confirm two other specific predictions. Contrary to our expectations, men with good mobility chances (in training) chose upward comparisons less often than did men with the poorest mobility chances. And highly mobile men, when they chose comparison persons who earn more than themselves, chose persons at higher occupational levels and persons outside Atlas more often than did those who have been barred from the training program. These unexpected results, combined with the data on present satisfaction, permit us to learn more than is contained in our original hypotheses about the influence of mobility chances on comparisons.

The fact that highly mobile men (in training) compare upward less often than others appears related to the finding that when highly mobile men do compare themselves to others earning more, they express greater *present* satisfaction with such comparisons. Both by comparing up less often and being *presently* satisfied with up comparisons, highly mobile men show contentment with their present wage position. These men express strong dissatisfaction only with the possibility of *remaining* below those chosen for comparison.

The other unexpected finding is the moderately high frequency with which highly mobile men chose upward comparisons of different status, rather than making more dissonant comparisons—to those earning more who are of similar status. This failure of the highly mobile group to choose more objectively dissonant comparisons appears also to be related to the moderately high *present* satisfaction of this group.

Our prediction that upwardly mobile men will be likely to choose upward comparisons (a prediction opposite to what the data show) was derived from the hypothesis that upwardly mobile men will be likely to choose potentially dissonant comparisons. This hypothesis was based largely on the assumption that upwardly mobile men wish to justify and legitimate a rise in status for themselves—and can accomplish this by pointing to dissonant comparisons. It may be, however, that we were mistaken in assuming that as mobility chances increase, a man will be more motivated to make a claim to a higher status. It may be, rather, that men whose mobility chances are *uncertain* would most feel the need to justify their advancement. Men whose promotion is possible, but uncertain, might use dissonant comparisons as a kind of graphic argument for their own promotion, just as a union negotiator in a bargaining session might point to wage inequities. At the present research site, those with the best opportunities for mobility, men in the training program, are relatively assured of their advancement. Such men do not have to "kick and holler" in order to be promoted. As long as they continue their training adequately, they will automatically rise. It may be, therefore, that it is not warranted to assume that men in the training program are motivated to justify and legitimate promotion for themselves. On the other hand, those who have been, so far, barred from the training program are much more uncertain about their promotion chances. Many of these men ("temporarily barred" group) believe they will have the opportunity to enter the program—but they cannot be sure. For those who will not get the chance to enter the training program, slow promotion outside the program is possible—but, again, uncertain. Under these circumstances, those barred from the training program may be motivated to "put up a fight" for promotion by pointing out the legitimacy of their claims for advancement. One way to do this is to make dissonant comparisons. In more general terms, our data suggest the possibility that dissonant comparisons are likely to be chosen by men who are uncertain about their advancement. This may be particularly true in situations where men perceive that protests may be effective in swaying those who control their status.

In addition to the motivatonal factors discussed, there may also be cognitive factors which help to explain why men in the training program chose more presently consonant comparisons than did men barred from the program. A great deal of information about the new training program was circulating through the refinery at the time of the research. Both men who had entered the program and those outside it were acutely aware that the program offered an opportunity for men to advance as far in three or four years as their predecessors had advanced in twenty years. There was also considerable discussion in the refinery about which trade groups would be offered training, which focused attention on the different opportunities available to different groups of workers. In these circumstances, it seems likely that the attention of men in the training program was directed to evidence of their being better off than particular other groups, while the attention of those barred from the program was directed to their being worse off than particular other groups. These facts suggest that a man's choice of comparisons is influenced not only by his objective position, relative to all others like himself, but also by the social circumstances which focus his attention on particular segments of those others.

Several other results, concerning present satisfaction with comparisons, are of special interest.

Men who have finished the training program chose a strikingly high proportion of objectively consonant comparisons—especially in their frequent choice of men at higher occupational levels when comparing upward. The fact that this group was also most satisfied at present with comparisons follows nicely our basic hypothesis concerning the relation of satisfaction to objective consonance.

Men who have not had a chance to enter the training program, and who therefore have poorer mobility chances, chose the most objectively dissonant comparisons. The more dissonant character of their comparisons is again paralleled by the lower *present* satisfaction of these groups. In fact, the ordering of groups on present satisfaction with comparisons corresponds closely to the ordering of groups on choice of dissonant comparisons—giving us added confidence in our basic theoretical framework.

Finally, it may be noted that among men now outside the training program who are presently satisfied with comparisons, those who expect to enter the training program in the future (Temporarily Barred group) are more likely to be *potentially* dissatisfied with upward comparisons than are those who do not expect to have this opportunity (Permanently Barred). This result follows the general finding that an increase in mobility chances leads to an increase in potential dissatisfaction.

6.2. Mobility Chances Outside the Company

Relation of Perceived Chances to Objective Chances. Having considered the relation between wage comparisons and mobility chances *inside* the company, we now turn to the relation between wage comparisons and mobility chances *outside Atlas.*

We are dealing, more specifically, with a rough measure of *perceived* chances, based on responses to the question: "Do you think you would ever be able to earn more *outside* Atlas than you're making here now?" Five fixed alternatives were provided following the question: (1) "There's a good chance I could make more outside Atlas," (2) "fair chance," (3) "slight chance," (4) "almost no chance," and (5) "I have no idea what my chances would be."

Although our measure is based on men's perceptions of their chances to earn more elsewhere, there is firm reason for believing that the answers to our question were based, for the main part, upon objective facts.

To check the realistic basis of perceived mobility chances, the following procedure was followed. Numerical values (as shown in Chapter 3) were assigned to each response to the question about earning more elsewhere except for "no idea" responses, which were omitted. Mean scores of perceived chances to earn more outside Atlas were then computed, separately for each occupational group within the refinery. Table 16 shows these mean scores.

Two occupational groups—men in the testing laboratory and men in mechanical trades—are most likely to believe they could earn more outside. Men in the laboratory are by far the best educated group in the refinery, and the youngest. They are also paid less than many other non-supervisory workers. These facts

TABLE 16. PERCEIVED CHANCES TO EARN MORE OUTSIDE ATLAS,[a] SEPARATELY FOR
MEN IN DIFFERENT OCCUPATIONAL GROUPS [b,c]

Occupational Group	Mean Score, Chances to Earn More Elsewhere	Number of Men
Laboratory	2.90	(21)
Mechanical department	3.20	(137)
Labor and janitorial	3.56	(27)
Miscellaneous (principally garage)	3.64	(25)
Operating process	3.78	(120)
Non-operating process	3.88	(49)
Total	3.51	(379)

[a] Low scores indicate good perceived chances to earn more elsewhere.
[b] Men who said they had "no idea" what their outside chances are (101), four men whose department was not identified, and three men who did not indicate their perceived chances to earn more elsewhere, are not included in this table.
[c] Solid line joining two mean scores indicates the difference is significant at the .01 level or beyond (2-tailed *t* test). Dashed line indicates difference significant at the .05 level (2-tailed *t* test). Broken line indicates difference significant at the .10 level (2-tailed *t* test).

provide a foundation for their belief that they can earn more elsewhere.

The difference in the mean scores of the two largest occupational groups—Mechanical Department and Operating Process Department—is of special interest.

Men in the Mechanical Department see significantly better opportunities elsewhere than do men in Operating Process. Mechanical Department men work at traditional trades like machinist, carpenter, mason which are potentially in demand in a great many industries. However, at Atlas, the top skill levels, and thus the top pay rates, for some of these trades have been closed off.

The picture in Operating Process is quite different. Men in this department, although similar to Mechanical men on such characteristics as education and age, have learned specialized skills which are of use nowhere but in an oil refinery. However, the top pay for their jobs exceeds the top pay rate of many Mechanical Department trades. Thus, we see that the difference between the two departments in perceived chances to earn more elsewhere is influenced by objective facts.

The relatively weak belief of men in Non-Operating Process, Labor and Janitorial, and Miscellaneous occupations in their ability to make more outside, also rests on fact. These men all do relatively unskilled work, for which Atlas pays better than do most other companies in the area.

Direction of Comparisons. Is there any relation between a man's perception of his chances to earn more outside and whether he chooses comparison persons who earn more or less than himself?

Table 17 shows that perceived chances to earn more outside have a tremendous impact on the direction of comparisons.

TABLE 17. DIRECTION OF COMPARISONS CHOSEN, SEPARATELY FOR MEN WITH DIFFERENT PERCEIVED CHANCES TO EARN MORE OUTSIDE ATLAS [a, b]

Perceived Chances to Earn More Elsewhere	Choose Comparison Persons Who Earn			Total (%)	Number of Men
	More Only (%)	Both More and Less (%)	Less Only (%)		
Good	59.1	27.3	13.6	100	(44)
Fair	42.5	44.8	12.6	100	(87)
Slight	24.6	53.9	21.5	100	(130)
Almost none	29.1	43.6	27.3	100	(110)
No idea	41.0	41.0	18.0	100	(100)

[a] Fifteen men who did not choose two comparisons are not included in this table.

[b] Solid line joining two percentages indicates the difference is significant at the .01 level (1-tailed test of percentage difference). Dashed line joinng two percentages indicates the difference is significant at the .05 level (1-tailed test of percentage difference).

Among those who think they have a good chance to earn more outside, 59 per cent choose for comparisons only persons who earn more than themselves. At the other extreme, among men who believe they have almost no chance to earn more outside, only 29 per cent choose only upward comparisons. Conversely, as perceived chances to earn more decrease, the proportion of comparisons only to those earning less, goes up. These results are in accord with hypothesis 5A.

The relationship between perceived chances to earn more and direction of wage comparisons holds up, even when differences in pay rate, in relative pay position, and in position vis-a-vis the training program are taken into account.

The one factor which appears to condition the relationship is the degree of social influence toward earning more (as indicated by responses to the question, "How often has anyone mentioned that a man like yourself deserves to be earning more money?" Table 18 shows that men who report strong social influences

TABLE 18. PERCENTAGE OF MEN WHO CHOOSE UPWARD COMPARISONS
EXCLUSIVELY, SEPARATELY FOR COMPARISONS CHOSEN BY
MEN WITH DIFFERENT PERCEIVED CHANCES TO EARN
MORE ELSEWHERE AND DIFFERENT DEGREES OF
SOCIAL INFLUENCE TO EARN MORE [a,b]
(Number of Comparers in Parentheses)

Perceived Chances to Earn More Elsewhere	Others Say Respondent Deserves More				Total (%)
	Quite Often (%)	Occa- sionally (%)	Once or Twice (%)	Never (%)	
Good or fair	60.7 (28)	56.5 (62)	⌈36.8 (19)	19.0 (21)	48.5 (130)
Slight or none	51.9 (27)	25.0 (88)	⌊25.0 (68)	19.3 (57)	26.7 (240)

[a] Men who said they had "no idea" what their chances are to earn more elsewhere (101), or who did not answer this question (4), or who did not choose two comparisons (15) are not included in this table.
[b] Solid line joining two percentages indicates the difference is significant at the .01 level or beyond (1-tailed test of percentage difference).

chose a large number of upward comparisons, regardless of their chances to earn more outside. And men who report least social influence did *not* often choose upward comparisons, regardless of their chances outside. Only when reported social influences are moderate (i.e., operate "occasionally") did mobility chances outside the company exert a marked effect on the direction of comparisons chosen.

This unanticipated result is difficult to interpret. It may be that social influences play an important role in determining a man's concern about, and thus alertness to, wage inequities. Where family and friends repeatedly say that a man should be earning more, he may become very alert to cases of persons who are earning more than himself—regardless of whether he believes he can earn more elsewhere. Where a man is confident that his family and associates believe he is doing well financially, or that they are not concerned about the matter, he may be much less concerned with and alert to problems of wage inequities—again, regardless of whether he can earn more outside. In the intermediate case, where he is exposed to "occasional" remarks by others that he should be earning more, the social definitions of his position may not be completely clear. In this situation, he may become concerned about, and alert to, wage inequities, only if the objective facts which he sees (i.e., opportunities elsewhere) justify such a concern. If this interpretation is correct, we would expect the choice of comparisons to be most influenced by mobility opportunities when the social definitions of a man's position are not completely clear and compelling.

Status of Comparisons Chosen. We expected that men with good mobility chances would not only be more likely to compare to those earning more than themselves, but that, when they chose upward comparisons, such comparisons would usually be dissonant.

Specifically, we predicted that men with good mobility chances, when comparing upward, would be more likely than others to choose comparisons of similar occupational status and at the same company.

Occupational level: Table 19 shows that, contrary to our prediction, men with good chances to earn more outside are more likely than others to choose upward comparisons at *higher* occupational levels than themselves (objectively consonant comparisons). They are especially more likely, when comparing upward, to choose professional men.

Place of work: We predicted that men with good mobility chances would more often choose upward comparison persons who work at the same company. However, there was little relation in the data between belief that one could earn more outside Atlas and the place of work of comparison persons chosen.

TABLE 19. OCCUPATIONAL LEVEL OF UPWARD COMPARISONS,[a] SEPARATELY FOR COMPARISONS CHOSEN BY MEN WITH DIFFERENT PERCEIVED CHANCES FOR EARNING MORE OUTSIDE ATLAS [b]

Choose Upward Comparisons Who Are	Think Chances to Earn More Elsewhere Are				
	Good (%)	Fair (%)	Slight (%)	None (%)	No Idea (%)
Professionals	23.1	19.2	16.4	7.4	7.4
Clerical, sales	5.1	5.1	1.9	3.7	4.9
Proprietors, managers ..	15.4	12.8	17.3	9.9	8.7
Blue-collar: foreman ..	12.8	9.0	17.3	12.3	12.4
Blue-collar: skilled or semiskilled	38.5	42.4	42.3	59.3	58.0
Other (farm; blue-collar, unspecified; etc.)	5.1	11.5	4.8	7.4	8.6
Total	100.0	100.0	100.0	100.0	100.0
Number of comparers ..	(39)	(78)	(104)	(81)	(81)

[a] Only the first upward comparison chosen by any respondent is included in this table. Four respondents who did not indicate their perception of their chances to earn more elsewhere are not included in this table.

[b] Dashed line between two percentages indicates the difference is significant at the .05 level (1-tailed test of percentage difference).

Before we attempt to interpret the meaning of these unanticipated findings concerning the relation of outside mobility chances to the status of upward comparisons chosen, it will be helpful to examine the relation between mobility chances outside the company and satisfaction with upward comparisons.

Present Satisfaction with Comparisons. Men who believe they can earn more outside Atlas compare "up" more often than do others. When they compare up, they are more likely than others to choose men of higher occupational levels. How satisfied are they with such upward comparisons?

Table 20 shows that as belief that one could earn more elsewhere increases, satisfaction with comparisons to those who earn more decreases. This general finding holds true regardless of relative pay position and regardless of position in the training program.

Potential Satisfaction with Comparisons. Those who think they could earn more elsewhere are more likely to be dissatisfied *at present* with the comparisons they make. The data show, moreover, that in those cases where such men are presently satisfied, they are more likely to be *potentially* dissatisfied.

Table 21 shows that, as perceived chances to earn more elsewhere increase, there is a steady and sizeable increase in dissatisfaction with the prospect of *continuing* to earn less than comparisons. This result is in accord with the prediction of hypothesis 6.

In a preceding section, it has been shown that good mobility chances *within* the company will also increase the likelihood of potential dissatisfaction with upward comparisons. Table 22 shows that *both* mobility chances within Atlas (position relative to training program) and mobility chances outside the company independently contribute to an increase in potential dissatisfaction with comparisons. At the extremes, those who are in the training program and who also could earn more outside Atlas

TABLE 20. PRESENT SATISFACTION WITH UPWARD COMPARISONS,[a] SEPARATELY FOR MEN WITH DIFFERENT PERCEIVED CHANCES TO EARN MORE OUTSIDE ATLAS [b]

Perceived Chances to Earn More Outside	Mean Present Satisfaction Score	Number of Men
Good	2.94	(39)
Fair	2.58	(76)
Slight	2.27	(104)
Almost none	2.36	(81)
No idea	2.45	(82)
Total	2.46	(382)

[a] Lower numbers indicate greater present satisfaction with upward comparisons.
[b] Solid line between two mean scores indicates the difference is significant at the .01 level (2-tailed t test). Dashed line indicates difference significant at the .05 level (2-tailed t test).

TABLE 21. SATISFACTION WITH PROSPECT OF CONTINUING TO EARN LESS THAN UPWARD COMPARISON PERSONS,[a] SEPARATELY FOR MEN WITH DIFFERENT PERCEIVED CHANCES TO EARN MORE OUTSIDE ATLAS [b]

Perceived Chances to Earn More Elsewhere	Mean "Potential" Satisfaction	Number of Comparers
Good	3.44	(26)
Fair	2.96	(65)
Slight	2.73	(97)
Almost none	2.46	(70)
No idea	2.59	(69)
Total	2.74	(327)

[a] Lower score indicates greater satisfaction with prospect of continuing to earn less.
[b] Solid line joining two means indicates the difference is significant at the .01 level (1-tailed t test). Dashed line joining two means indicates the difference is significant at the .05 level (1-tailed t test).

TABLE 22. MEAN "POTENTIAL" SATISFACTION SCORES,[a] SEPARATELY FOR MEN WITH DIFFERENT PERCEIVED CHANCES TO EARN MORE OUTSIDE ATLAS AND IN DIFFERENT POSITIONS VIS-À-VIS COMPANY TRAINING PROGRAM [b, c]
(Number of Comparers in Parentheses)

Perceived Chances to Earn More Elsewhere	Training Program Position			
	In Now	Finished	Tempo-rarily Barred	Perma-nently Barred
Good or fair	3.38 (32)	3.07 (15)	2.68 (14)	2.80 (10)
Slight or none	2.87 (50)	2.40 (20)	2.68 (22)	2.36 (45)

[a] Lower scores indicate greater satisfaction with the prospect of continuing to earn less than comparison persons.

[b] Fifty-eight respondents who were presently satisfied with upward comparisons, but who said they had "no idea" of their chances to earn more elsewhere, are not included in this table.

[c] Dashed line joining two means indicates the difference is significant at the .05 level (1-tailed *t* test). Broken line joining two means indicates the difference is significant at the .10 level (1-tailed *t* test).

are most dissatisfied with the prospect of remaining below comparison persons; men who are permanently barred from the training program and who believe they could not earn more outside Atlas are most satisfied with the prospect of remaining below comparison persons.

There is, however, an important difference between the comparisons chosen by men with good outside-the-company mobility chances and persons chosen by men with good inside-the-company mobility chances. We have pointed out in the previous section of this chapter that men in the company training program are likely to focus on the greater seniority, experience, or age of comparison persons. Such comparisons stress potential dissonance since the comparer's position on these dimensions will improve, and he will be entitled to earn as much as the comparison person is earning now.

However, those men who perceive good *outside* mobility chances and who are presently satisfied with upward comparisons do not often mention seniority, experience, or age differences as reasons for their present satisfaction.

We have seen that good mobility chances either inside or outside the company lead to greater dissatisfaction with the prospect of remaining lower than comparison persons. The present data suggest, however, that those whose chances lie within the company choose often as comparison persons men in whose footsteps they will be following (i.e., those with more seniority and experience) while those whose mobility chances lie outside the company are not able to make this kind of comparison. Many of them are not following a path in the footsteps of others. And although they hope to catch up to the comparison persons, there is more separating them than time in the form of seniority, age, and experience. We may, then, revise hypothesis 5 as follows: Men who have good chances for upward mobility along a prescribed career path are likely to make potentially dissonant comparisons to those ahead of them on this path.

Special Characteristics of Men with Good Outside Mobility Chances. Most of the data concerning the effect of mobility chances outside Atlas on wage comparisons have supported our hypotheses. Men who believe they can earn more outside are more likely to choose upward comparisons. When they choose upward comparisons, they are more likely to be presently dissatisfied with the comparisons. When they are presently satisfied, they are more likely to be *potentially* dissatisfied than are those who think they cannot earn more elsewhere.

Yet there is one serious discrepancy in our data. When men with good outside mobility chances choose upward comparisons, they are more likely than others to choose persons at a higher occupational level. Such upward comparisons—to those earning more but of higher general status—appear to be relatively consonant. Yet men with good outside mobility chances are most dissatisfied with upward comparisons. This result appears contrary to an element of our basic theoretical framework—that those who make objectively consonant comparisons (e.g., to persons earning more but at higher occupational levels) are more likely than others to be satisfied with the comparisons they make. How are the data concerning outside mobility chances to be explained?

One possible explanation is that, contrary to our theoretical framework, highly mobile men are more often dissatisfied with upward comparisons *because* they often choose upward comparisons at higher occupational levels.

The data show, however, that this explanation must be rejected. When highly mobile men choose upward comparisons at higher occupational levels, they are more satisfied with the comparisons than when they choose upward comparisons at their own occupational levels. In other words, the present dissatisfaction of the highly mobile group is occurring *in spite of,* and not because of, the many objectively consonant comparisons which they make.

A more fruitful approach is to ask whether highly mobile men have special characteristics which would lead them to choose comparisons at higher occupational levels. It turns out that men who perceive good chances to earn more outside are much better educated than are those who see little chance to do better elsewhere (see Table 23). It seems probable that the greater education of the highly mobile group would tend to produce within this group more comparisons to persons of higher status, since persons like themselves are often at higher occupational levels, and since, therefore, they are more likely than poorly educated men to associate with those of higher occupational levels.

The special composition of the highly mobile group also helps to explain their strong dissatisfaction with comparisons to persons who earn more than themselves. Among men who choose comparisons at higher occupational levels, the upwardly mobile men are less likely than others to see a great educational difference between themselves and the comparison persons. Among men who choose comparison persons at the same occupational level, the highly mobile comparers are more likely than others to see themselves as better educated than the comparison persons. In both of these cases, highly mobile men have more reason than others to be dissatisfied with comparisons to persons who earn more than themselves.

TABLE 23. EDUCATION OF RESPONDENTS, SEPARATELY FOR MEN WITH DIFFERENT PERCEIVED CHANCES TO EARN MORE OUTSIDE ATLAS [a, b]

Perceived Chances to Earn More Elsewhere	Educational Level			Total (%)	Number of men
	Eighth Grade or Lower (%)	Some High School (%)	Completed High School or Beyond (%)		
Good	22.0	39.0	39.0	100	(41)
Fair	29.3	45.1	25.6	100	(82)
Slight	33.6	37.6	28.8	100	(125)
Almost none	57.0	26.3	16.7	100	(114)
No idea	58.0	26.0	16.0	100	(100)
Total	42.7	33.8	23.4	100	(462)

[a] Twenty-seven men who did not indicate their education or their perceived chances to earn more elsewhere are not included in this table.
[b] Solid line joining two percentages indicates the difference is significant at the .01 level (1-tailed test of percentage difference). Dashed line indicates difference is significant at .05 level (1-tailed test of percentage difference).

6.3. Summary and Conclusions

In order to better evaluate hypotheses 5 and 6, it is useful to compare the effects of mobility chances *within* Atlas and *outside* Atlas on the choice of comparisons and on satisfaction with comparisons.

One major difference in the effect of these two aspects of mobility chances is that good mobility chances *within* Atlas led to *fewer* upward comparisons, while good mobility chances *outside* Atlas led to *more* upward comparisons (Tables 9 and 17).

A second major difference is that good chances to earn more outside Atlas resulted in greater *present* dissatisfaction with comparisons, while good mobility chances within the company did not lead to more present discontent (Tables 13 and 20).

The importance of mobility chances within the company lay principally in their latent, long-term effect on wage comparisons. Men who had good mobility chances within Atlas often focused on *potentially* dissonant features of upward comparisons and, when presently satisfied, were likely to be discontented with the prospect of *remaining* lower than comparison persons. Those who perceive good mobility chances outside Atlas also were more likely than others to be *potentially* dissatisfied with wage comparisons, but the *potential* dissatisfaction of this group was in addition to, not instead of, a greater likelihood of *present* dissatisfaction.

These differences between the effects of mobility chances inside and outside the company make it necessary for us to re-examine our thinking about the effects of mobility chances on comparisons. We expected that men who saw a chance for higher status would lay claim to such status as quickly as possible, by making dissonant comparisons. In making this assumption, we did not distinguish between mobility chances inside and outside the company.

But the advancement opportunities within and outside Atlas have some important practical and conceptional differences. Advancement in the training program at Atlas is relatively assured. Certain specified training and experience, and the passing of objective examinations, qualify a man for a raise in job classification and a raise in pay. Moreover, the company has committed itself and is making active efforts to help the men in the program to advance in skill and status. Under these conditions, men with the best mobility chances (those in the training program) do not have to struggle for advancement. If we consider the choice of dissonant comparisons as providing justification for advance-

ment, it appears that men in the training program have little
need to provide such justification.

What we have called mobility chances outside the company
(i.e., chance to earn more outside) constitutes an entirely different situation in the certainty and ease with which promotion can
be accomplished. If men who can earn more outside expect to
use this fact as ammunition in a quest for higher wages at Atlas,
then they will have to make their present "inequitable" position
known far and wide. Even if they expect to advance by actually
leaving Atlas, they need to keep the picture of their present low
status before themselves as an incentive to seeking a better position. In short, for men whose mobility chances lie primarily in
the fact that they can earn more elsewhere, the choice of dissonant comparisons can provide a needed justification and legiti-
mation for seeking a rise in status.

This interpretation is consistent also with the fact that men
who have been barred from the training program chose dissonant
comparisons more often than did men currently in the program.
Like men who believe they can earn more elsewhere, those who
have not been given the chance to enter the training program
have no assurance that they will be advanced in job classification
or in wages. Men in both of these categories may well feel the
need to make a strong case in favor of their advancement—to
the company, to the worker representatives who negotiate with
the company, and to themselves. Such a need to justify advancement would be served by the choice of dissonant comparisons.

The present data have indicated that it is not the probability
of mobility as such which leads to the choice of dissonant comparisons. It may be, rather, that when mobility is *possible but
not assured,* and when the individual believes he can have some
direct or indirect influence on the final outcome, he will be motivated to make dissonant comparisons.

It may be also that "best mobility chances" within Atlas and
"best mobility chances" outside the company produce different
cognitive effects, which help to account for their differential

influence on wage comparisons. To have the best mobility chances within the company means to be in the training program. This, in turn, means having one's attention focused on others inside and outside the company who have not had similar good fortune. The effect of being able to earn more elsewhere is opposite. In such circumstances, one's attention is likely to be caught by others like himself who are earning more, but whose job he could fill. Thus, situations which may both be labeled situations of "good mobility chances" focus the individual's attention on very different kinds of wage comparisons. When good mobility chances are evident to the individual in the context of others doing better than himself, he is likely to choose dissonant comparisons. When good mobility chances are evident to the individual in the context of others' chances being worse, then he is likely to choose consonant comparisons.

CHAPTER 7

Acceptance of Personal Responsibility

In discussing the influence of relative pay position and of mobility chances on the choice of wage comparisons, it has been illuminating at certain points to hold constant men's feelings of personal responsibility for their position. We turn now to a direct consideration of the effect that acceptance or non-acceptance of personal responsibility has on wage comparisons. We wish, first, to check hypothesis 7, that "men who see the responsibility for their occupational position as *not* being their own will be more likely to choose dissonant wage comparisons."

7.1. Direction of Comparison

We predicted first (hypothesis 7A) that "non-responsible" men will more often choose comparisons who earn more than themselves. Table 24 shows that this prediction is *not* supported. How much personal responsibility a man accepts had little influence on how often he chose comparisons above or below himself in earnings.

Even when we hold constant (in turn) training program position and relative pay position, acceptance of responsibility bears little relation to the direction of comparisons.

TABLE 24. DIRECTION OF COMPARISONS CHOSEN, SEPARATELY FOR MEN WHO ACCEPT DIFFERENT DEGREES OF PERSONAL RESPONSIBILITY [a]

| Responsibility Accepted | Choose Comparison Persons Who Earn | | | Total (%) | Number of Comparers |
	More Only (%)	Both More and Less (%)	Less Only (%)		
Little	34.6	47.5	17.9	100	(179)
Moderate	33.5	46.2	20.3	100	(158)
Great	39.6	39.6	20.9	100	(134)

[a] Fifteen men who did not choose two comparisons and three men who did not answer both items of the personal responsibility index are not included in this table.

7.2. Status of Comparison Persons

Occupational Level. Among men who choose upward comparisons, those who accept great personal responsibility for their fate are somewhat more likely to choose comparisons at higher occupational levels (consonant comparisons). This relation is small and, though in the direction predicted (hypothesis 7B), is statistically non-significant.

However, among men who stand relatively low on pay, perception of responsibility makes a more marked difference (see Table 25). Among men who are relatively low on pay and accept little responsibility for their low position, 68 per cent chose upward comparisons at their own occupational level (dissonant comparisons) while only 5 per cent chose upward comparisons who are professional men. Among men who also stand relatively low on pay but who accept great personal responsibility for their position, only 40 per cent chose upward comparisons at their own occupational level and 19 per cent chose upward comparisons who are professional persons (consonant comparisons). Those who accept great responsibility also chose upward comparisons in miscellaneous "other" occupations (principally farm occupations) more often than did men who accept little responsibility. Comparison to men in miscellaneous *different* occupations is, like the choice of professionals, more objectively consonant than comparison to men of the *same* occupational category who are earning more than oneself.

These data indicate that it is necessary for a man to be *both* doing relatively poorly on wages and rejecting responsibility for his poor fate before he will make dissonant comparisons. It is likely that this outcome results from the fact that dissonant comparisons have a different meaning to individuals who have different perceptions of who is responsible for their poor position. For the man who thinks he himself is primarily responsible for his fate, dissonant comparisons indicate failure. Such comparisons are painful and are therefore likely to be avoided. But for the man who sees his low position as being caused by others, dissonant comparisons can serve both as a protest and as a means of raising his legitimate status in his own eyes and in the view of others.

Place of Work. One way in which men who reject personal responsibility for their fate choose more dissonant comparisons is to choose men of their own occupational level who earn more than themselves. We predicted (hypothesis 7B) that another specific way in which such men would make dissonant comparisons would be to choose upward comparisons who work for the same company. However, there was little relation between acceptance of personal responsibility and the place of work of comparison persons chosen.

7.3. Satisfaction with Upward Comparisons

We have seen that whether men accept little or great personal responsibility or not has little effect on whether they choose comparison persons above or below themselves in earnings. But when

TABLE 25. OCCUPATIONAL LEVEL OF UPWARD COMPARISONS,[a] SEPARATELY FOR PERSONS CHOSEN BY MEN WHO ACCEPT DIFFERENT DEGREES OF PERSONAL RESPONSIBILITY AND WHO ARE IN DIFFERENT RELATIVE PAY POSITIONS [b]

Relative Pay Position	Responsibility Accepted	Occupational Level of "Up" Comparison						Total (%)
		Prof. (%)	Cleric. Sales (%)	Mgr.-Prop. (%)	Blue-Collar Foreman (%)	Blue-Collar Skilled, Semi-Skilled (%)	Other [c] (%)	
Low	Little (N = 62)	4.8	1.6	16.1	9.7	67.7	0.0	100
	Moderate (N = 68)	8.8	2.9	4.4	16.2	57.4	10.3	100
	Great (N = 52)	19.2	0.0	11.5	13.5	40.4	15.4	100
Medium	Little (N = 40)	15.0	5.0	17.5	5.0	55.0	2.5	100
	Moderate (N = 27)	14.8	3.7	18.5	7.4	40.7	14.8	100
	Great (N = 17)	5.9	11.8	5.9	29.4	47.1	0.0	100
High	Little (N = 45)	22.2	6.7	13.3	15.6	37.8	4.4	100
	Moderate (N = 33)	15.2	6.1	15.2	18.2	42.4	3.0	100
	Great (N = 37)	21.6	2.7	16.2	10.8	35.1	13.5	100

[a] For each respondent, only the first upward comparison is included in this table. Six respondents who did not answer both personal responsibility questions are not included in this table.

[b] Solid line joining two percentages indicates the difference is significant at the .01 level (1-tailed tests except "Other" column, where 2-tailed test was used, since difference was not specifically predicted). Dashed line indicates the difference is significant at the .05 level (1-tailed test, except in "Mgr.-Proprietor" column, where difference was not predicted).

[c] Includes primarily comparison persons in farm occupations and in occupations which could not be sufficiently identified. Also included in "Other" are unskilled or unemployed.

men *do* choose upward comparisons, is their satisfaction with such comparisons affected by their perceptions about responsibility?

Table 8 shows that, in accordance with hypothesis 8, men who accept great responsibility for their position are more satisfied with comparisons to those who earn more than themselves. However, this table also shows that acceptance of responsibility affects satisfaction only among men who are relatively low on pay. Again, it is the *combination* of being relatively low on pay and rejecting personal responsibility which results in dissatisfaction with upward comparisons. This result is consistent with the finding that the combination of low relative position and rejection of responsibility leads to the choice of objectively dissonant comparisons (men of similar occupational status who are earning more).

The influence of perceptions of personal responsibility is also conditioned by men's position vis-a-vis the training program. (Training program position is essentially independent of relative pay position.) Table 26 shows that rejection of personal responsibility is strongly associated with dissatisfaction concerning comparisons only among men who have been barred, either temporarily or permanently, from the company training program.

As long as men are doing well, then, either in present earnings relative to others or in prospects for future advancement, they are satisfied with upward comparisons, regardless of whether they accept personal responsibility. But when their fortunes are not going so well, as reflected by relatively low present earnings or by being frozen out of the training program, acceptance of personal responsibility has a marked effect on satisfaction. If men are doing poorly in some respect and blame others rather than themselves, they will be dissatisfied about earning less than comparison persons.

7.4. Summary and Conclusions

The results reported in this chapter show that acceptance of personal responsibility has a different influence on comparisons than do other variables considered so far.

TABLE 26. MEAN PRESENT SATISFACTION [a] WITH UPWARD COMPARISONS, SEPARATELY
FOR MEN WHO ARE IN DIFFERENT POSITIONS VIS-À-VIS COMPANY TRAINING
PROGRAM AND WHO ACCEPT DIFFERENT DEGREES OF PERSONAL
RESPONSIBILITY [b]

(Number of Comparers in Parentheses)

Training Program Position	Comparer Accepts			Total
	Little Respon-sibility	Mod-erate Respon-sibility	Great Respon-sibility	
In program	⌈2.43	2.42	2.33	2.40
	¦(41)	(40)	(29)	(110)
Temporarily barred	⌊2.89	2.40	2.43	2.57
	(19)	(29)	(21)	(60)
Permanently barred	2.71	2.46	2.35	2.55
	(46)	(25)	(24)	(95)

[a] Lower scores indicate greater present satisfaction with upward comparisons.
[b] Broken line joining two means indicates the difference is significant at the .10 level
(1-tailed t test for groups differing in acceptance of responsibility; 2-tailed test for
groups differing in training program position).

Relative pay position, mobility chances inside the company,
and mobility chances outside the company all make a difference
in how often men choose comparison persons who earn more
than themselves. In each case, men who are disadvantaged in
some way—by being low in relative pay, by being barred from
the training program, or by earning less at Atlas than they think
they can earn elsewhere—are more likely than others to compare
upward. But perceptions of personal responsibility have no effect
on the direction of comparisons. Whether a man compares "up"
or "down" appears, then, to be influenced by what his position is
—not by whom he sees as responsible for it.

But given a certain likelihood of a man comparing upward,
by virtue of his present and anticipated position, perceptions of
responsibility appear to make a big difference in the kind of upward comparisons made and in satisfaction with such comparisons. Those who are induced by their present poor position to

compare upward, but who feel personally responsible for their fate, are likely to try to make the upward comparisons more palatable (consonant) by such devices as choosing professional men. And they are more likely to be satisfied with the upward comparisons.

In this discussion, acceptance of responsibility has been treated as an independent variable and comparisons as dependent. This approach seems plausible in view of the fact that the items of the personal responsibility index concern relatively long-lived, enduring perceptions, while the specific wage comparisons were elicited on the spur of the moment.

However, the possibility of reciprocal causation over time should be reiterated. It may be that, in some cases, making dissonant comparisons leads to a rejection of personal responsibility. The direction of causation is not, however, crucial for the argument here. The essential point is that, whichever occurs first, dissonant comparisons will not long be chosen and dissatisfaction not long maintained unless personal responsibility for the situation is rejected.

CHAPTER 8

Social Influences

In the early thinking that preceded this research, the writer placed great theoretical emphasis upon the influence of important membership groups (e.g., immediate family, old school friends) on the choice of wage comparisons. The essential idea was that a man would tend to accept as a standard of comparison those persons or groups whom his own membership groups used as a standard against which to judge him. However, despite extensive probing in exploratory interviews, respondents reported little discussion of wage comparisons in their families or in other membership groups, and few explicit attempts by relatives or friends to specify appropriate comparisons for them. Instead, factors closer to the work situation—relative pay position, mobility chances, and acceptance of personal responsibility for one's position—appeared to be more important as determinants of comparisons.

Still, it was felt that influence from other people would make some difference in wage comparisons. Accordingly, the following question was included in our questionnaire: "How often has anyone mentioned that a man like yourself deserves to be earning more money?" Each man had a choice of four check-list alternatives: "It has happened quite often," ". . . occasionally," ". . . once or twice," "It has never happened."

8.1. Limitations of the Measure of Social Influence

Although it was hoped that this question would reflect the degree of social influences brought to bear on a person, it seems likely that it is not a good measure of actual social influence. Whether a man reports that others say he deserves to earn more probably is related to his own appraisal of whether he deserves more. Men who feel underpaid are probably more likely to bring up this subject with others—and thus provoke remarks that they deserve more. Furthermore, men who themselves feel they deserve more are probably more likely to selectively remember the remarks of others which support their own point of view.

However, in spite of the weakness of our measure of social influence, we may treat it as a very rough indicator of actual social influence. Though we need to interpret our data cautiously, the results involving the measure are of interest.

Hypothesis 9 states that "men who are told by others that they deserve to be earning more will often choose dissonant comparisons." Let us see how this prediction fared.

8.2. Direction of Comparison

Table 27 shows that as reported social influences to earn more increase, the proportion of upward comparisons also increases sharply and steadily. Among those who report that no one has ever said they deserve more, only one out of four men chose only upward comparisons, while another one-fourth chose only downward comparisons. At the other extreme, among men who report that others have "quite often" said they deserve more money, well over one-half chose upward comparisons exclusively, while only one man in twelve chose exclusively downward comparisons.

Men who report social influence to earn more are more likely to choose upward comparisons even when we hold constant (in

TABLE 27. DIRECTION OF COMPARISONS CHOSEN, SEPARATELY FOR MEN WHO REPORT DIFFERENT DEGREES OF SOCIAL INFLUENCE TO EARN MORE [a, b]

Others Say Respondent Deserves More	Choose Comparison Persons Who Earn			Total (%)	Number of Comparers
	More Only (%)	Both More and Less (%)	Less Only (%)		
Often	56.3	35.2	8.5	100	(71)
Occasionally	37.9	46.3	15.8	100	(190)
Once or twice	28.8	42.3	28.8	100	(111)
Never	25.7	49.5	24.8	100	(101)

[a] Men who did not choose two comparisons (15) or who did not answer the question about social influences (1) are not included in this table.

[b] Solid line joining two percentages indicates the difference is significant at the .01 level (1-tailed test of percentage difference). Broken line indicates difference is significant at the .10 level (1-tailed test of percentage difference).

turn) relative pay position, actual pay rate, training program position, perception of chances to earn more elsewhere, and acceptance of personal responsibility. These data support hypothesis 9A.

8.3. Status of Comparison Persons

Occupational Level. The data show that, among men who choose upward comparisons, those who report strong social influence to earn more are less likely to choose professional men as upward comparisons (see Table 28). The upward comparisons of those experiencing strong social influence are therefore, as expected, more objectively dissonant than the upward comparisons of those reporting little influence.

Place of Work. Table 29 shows that men who report a complete absence of social influence to earn more are less likely than others to choose upward comparisons at the same company. This result is in accord with the prediction that men who experience little social influence to earn more will choose more consonant comparisons. However, there is not a linear relation between reported social influences and the choice of upward comparisons who work at Atlas. Men who report social influence quite often, occasionally, or only once or twice choose upward comparisons at the same company about equally often. Only at the extreme, where a complete lack of social influence to earn more is reported, do comparisons to Atlas men fall off.

TABLE 28. OCCUPATIONAL LEVEL OF UPWARD COMPARISONS, SEPARATELY FOR MEN WHO REPORT DIFFERENT DEGREES OF SOCIAL INFLUENCE TO EARN MORE [a, b]

Occupational Level of "Up" Comparisons	Others Say Respondent Deserves More			
	Often (%)	Occasionally (%)	Once or Twice (%)	Never (%)
Professional	10.6	11.0	16.3	19.5
Clerical, sales	13.6	14.1	7.5	13.0
Proprietor, manager	3.0	4.3	2.5	5.2
Blue-collar: foreman	15.2	11.0	13.8	15.6
Blue-collar: skilled, semi-skilled	54.6	50.3	51.3	39.0
Other (farm; blue-collar, unspecified; etc.)	3.0	9.2	8.8	7.8
Total	100.0	100.0	100.0	100.0
Number of comparers	(66)	(163)	(80)	(77)

[a] For any respondent, only the first upward comparison made is included in this table. One man did not answer the question about social influence.
[b] Broken line joining two percentages indicates the difference is significant at the .10 level (1-tailed test of percentage difference).

The general finding that low social influence to earn more is associated with fewer upward comparisons in the same company must be qualified. The complete absence of social influence leads to a drop in upward comparisons to those in the same company

TARLE 29. PLACE OF WORK OF UPWARD COMPARISON PERSONS, SEPARATELY FOR MEN WHO REPORT DIFFERENT DEGREES OF SOCIAL INFLUENCE TO EARN MORE [a, b]

Others Say Respondent Deserves More	Upward Comparison Persons Work		Total (%)	Number of Comparers
	At Atlas (%)	Outside Atlas (%)		
Often	37.3	62.8	100	(51)
Occasionally	43.9	56.1	100	(132)
Once or twice	40.3	59.7	100	(57)
Never	25.0	75.0	100	(60)
Total	38.3	61.7	100	(300)

[a] Only men who chose an upward comparison whose place of work could be identified are included in this table. For any respondent, only one upward comparison is included.
[b] Solid line joining two percentages indicates the difference is significant at the .01 level (1-tailed test of percentage difference). Dashed line indicates the difference is significant at the .05 level (1-tailed test of percentage difference).

only when relative pay position is medium or high (see Table 30). Men who are relatively low on pay chose a large proportion of upward comparisons at Atlas regardless of whether others say they deserve more.

This result suggests that men are not likely to focus their attention on dissonant comparisons unless there is some kind of reality, either objective or social, which brings such comparisons to their attention. Where the objective reality is that men are doing relatively well on earnings compared to others, they will not often choose dissonant comparisons unless there is a social reality which defines their position as poorer than it should be.

8.4. Satisfaction with Upward Comparisons

Since men who report social influences to earn more often choose objectively dissonant upward comparisons, we would expect them to be often dissatisfied with upward comparisons.

Table 31 shows this expectation (expressed in hypothesis 10) to be supported. As men report more social influence to earn more, there is a steady and marked decrease in satisfaction with upward comparisons.

Social influence to earn more brings a decrease in satisfaction regardless of men's relative pay position. However, the effect of social influences is most marked among men who stand relatively low in pay. The combination of low relative pay position and social support for the belief that one deserves more leads to the greatest dissatisfaction with upward comparisons. This re-

TABLE 30. PERCENTAGE OF UPWARD COMPARISONS WHO WORK AT ATLAS,
SEPARATELY FOR PERSONS CHOSEN BY MEN REPORTING DIFFERENT
DEGREES OF SOCIAL INFLUENCE TO EARN MORE, AND IN
DIFFERENT RELATIVE PAY POSITIONS [a, b]
(Number of Comparers in Parentheses)

Others Say Respondent Deserves More	Respondent's Relative Pay Position		
	Low (%)	Medium (%)	High (%)
Often	32.3 (31)	50.0 (14)	33.3 (6)
Occasionally	46.6 (58)	44.0 (25)	⌐40.8 ⏐(49)
Once or twice	40.7 (27)	25.0 (16)	⏐57.1 ⏐(14)
Never	38.5 (26)	18.2 (11)	⌐13.0 (23)

[a] For any respondent, only the first upward comparison whose place of work was identified is included in this table.
[b] Dashed line joining two percentages indicates difference is significant at the .05 level (1-tailed test of percentage difference).

sult is not consistent with the finding that those who are relatively low on pay choose dissonant upward comparisons (persons who work at Atlas), regardless of the extent of social influence to earn more. It may be that although low relative pay position induces men to make objectively dissonant comparisons, the support of others is necessary to trigger expression of the dissatisfaction that accompanies dissonance.

TABLE 31. MEAN SATISFACTION WITH UPWARD COMPARISONS,[a] SEPARATELY FOR MEN WHO REPORT DIFFERENT DEGREES OF SOCIAL INFLUENCE TO EARN MORE [b, c]

Others Say Respondent Deserves More	Mean Satisfaction Score	Number of Comparers
Often	3.05	(65)
Occasionally	2.53	(162)
Once or twice	2.19	(80)
Never	2.08	(77)
Total	2.46	(384)

[a] Lower scores indicate greater satisfaction with upward comparisons.
[b] For any respondent, only the first upward comparison is included in this table. Men who chose no upward comparisons or who did not indicate their degree of satisfaction are omitted from this table.
[c] Solid line joining two percentages indicates difference is significant at the .01 level (1-tailed t test).

8.5. Summary

The probable limitations of our measure of social influences to earn more have been noted, but the measure may be tentatively accepted as a rough indicator of actual social influence. As reported social influence to earn more increases, there is a sharp increase in the proportion of upward comparisons.

As social influence to earn more increases, there is also an increase in the choice of objectively dissonant comparisons (i.e., the choice of men of similar occupational status and same place of work who earn more). The increase in choice of dissonant comparisons is paralleled by an increased dissatisfaction with comparisons among men reporting strong social influence to earn more. In general, the hypotheses concerning the effect of social influences on comparisons are supported.

CHAPTER 9

Summary and Conclusions

9.1. The Nature of Comparisons

We began this inquiry by asking the question: What determines a man's choice of wage comparisons?

Before we could attempt to explain differences in the comparisons that various groups of men make, it was necessary to categorize the great diversity of concrete wage comparisons into conceptually meaningful *types*. We distinguished two components of a wage comparison—the relative standing of the two persons on earnings and the relative status of the two persons on dimensions related to earnings. By considering whether a difference in earnings was likely to be perceived as consonant with, or dissonant with, other differences between the two persons, we arrived at the concepts of consonant wage comparisons and dissonant wage comparisons.

A perceived dissonant wage comparison was defined as one in which the comparer perceives the difference in earnings between himself and the comparison person as inappropriate to, or incongruent with, other relevant differences between the two persons. An objectively dissonant wage comparison was defined as one in which the objective differences between the two persons are culturally considered incongruent with, or inappropriate to, the difference in earnings.

We predicted that men who choose objectively dissonant comparisons (e.g., comparison persons of *similar* status who earn more than themselves) will be more often dissatisfied with comparisons than will men who choose objectively consonant comparisons (e.g., comparison persons of *different* status who earn more than themselves). Some support for this prediction came from the findings that satisfaction with comparisons to those earning more, increased when the comparison persons were different in occupational level (e.g., professionals) or in place of work. Contrary to our expectation, however, respondents expressed greater satisfaction with comparisons to close relatives who earn more than themselves than with comparisons to non-relatives earning more than themselves. It seems likely that this result reflects people's reluctance to express those feelings of discontent which might be labeled as morally wrong, although there is no quantitative evidence bearing on this interpretation.

Another way in which the relation of dissonance and satisfaction was studied was to examine the reasons men gave for feeling satisfied or dissatisfied with comparisons. Our prediction that men would subjectively link satisfaction with consonance and dissatisfaction with dissonance found support in the data. Most men who are satisfied with comparisons to those who earn more than themselves explained their satisfaction in terms of some other difference between themselves and the comparison person (e.g., skill, seniority, type of work) which makes the wage difference appropriate (or consonant). Most men who are dissatisfied about earning less than comparison persons gave as reasons their equality with or superiority to the comparison person in some important way which makes the wage difference inappropriate (or dissonant).

These data indicate that the "direction" of a wage comparison (i.e., whether or not the comparison person is earning more than the comparer) is meaningful to individuals only in the context of relative standing on other status attributes. These data indicate, therefore, that in order to fruitfully categorize wage comparisons we must consider *simultaneously* differences in earnings and differences in other related attributes. The perceived congruence of the wage difference and other status differences is what makes the comparisons appear consonant or dissonant to those doing the comparing.

The fruitfulness of the present way of categorizing comparisons is indicated also by the fact that we were able to find many consistent and meaningful differences between groups in the choice of objectively consonant and dissonant comparisons.

9.2. Relative Wage Position

Our results indicate that men's wage position relative to those like themselves (in age, seniority, education, and family) is an important determinant of the comparisons they choose, while their absolute wage position (pay rate) has, in itself, little influence on the choice of comparisons. Men whose earnings are lower than most others like themselves tended to make dissonant comparisons (to those on their own occupational level who are earning more). Men who stand relatively low on earnings are also more dissatisfied than others with the comparisons they made. These data concerning the influence of relative and absolute wage position support the interpretations of *The American Soldier* researches.

There is evidence, however, that a man's objective position relative to others like himself is not sufficient in itself to account for his choice of wage comparisons. Those who are doing relatively poorly on earnings will not often choose dissonant comparisons and be dissatisfied with comparisons unless they reject personal responsibility for their present position. Similarly, those who reject personal responsibility for their fate will not choose dissonant comparisons and be dissatisfied unless they are doing relatively poorly on pay. Both the objective fact (and presumably the perception) of doing poorly on wages and the rejection of personal responsibility for this fate are necessary in order for dissonant comparisons to occur frequently.

It seems likely that acceptance or rejection of personal responsibility makes a big difference in the motivation of low-earners to choose dissonant comparisons. For those who accept responsibility for their present position, dissonant comparisons may lead to feelings of personal failure. Moreover, such men cannot use such comparisons as evidence that they deserve higher earnings. But low-earners who blame others (such as their employer) for their present position can use dissonant comparisons as a protest and as a claim to higher status. Such a claim to higher status may be intended to persuade others and may also serve to bolster their own self-esteem.

Another factor which interacts with relative pay position is the extent to which the individual has been set on the road to advancement in status and earnings. Men who stand relatively low in present earnings but who have been given the opportunity to enter a training program which almost guarantees a progressive rise in status and wages did not often choose upward (dissonant) comparisons. Similarly, men who have been barred from the training program but who already relatively stand high on wages did not often choose dissonant comparisons. Only when the *combination* of low relative earnings and the lack of clear opportunity to raise one's position were both present, did a big jump in the choice of dissonant comparisons occur.

The fact that only those low-earners who have not been given a chance to improve themselves often chose dissonant comparisons suggests that these comparisons represent an attempt to achieve recognition by others of their "rightful" claim to a higher status—as well as to reinforce their own self-esteem. Men in a similar relative wage position whose status aspirations are being directly recognized and aided through the training program did not need to stress the appropriateness of their being granted a higher status. Their claims have already been recognized and something is being done about these claims.

The interaction of relative pay position, both with acceptance of personal responsibility and with mobility opportunities, indicates that low relative position, which confronts individuals with many dissonant comparisons, will actually lead to the choice of dissonant comparisons only when other conditions in the situation produce motivation for such comparisons. The fact that rejection of personal responsibility and the lack of clear mobility paths both facilitate dissonant comparisons suggests that the motivation of achieving recognition of a claim to higher status is important in producing such comparisons.

9.3. Mobility Chances

We predicted that as men's mobility chances improve, they will more often choose potentially dissonant comparisons and will more often be dissatisfied with the prospect of remaining below comparison persons in wages. These predictions found some support in the data. Among men who chose comparison persons who earn more than themselves, those comparers with the best within-company mobility chances were, as predicted, most likely to focus on the greater seniority, age, or experience of comparison persons as justifying the present difference in wages. Since all comparers will, with time, attain greater seniority, age, and experience, those who focused on this type of difference between themselves and those who earn more were spotlighting the elements of potential dissonance in their comparisons. Consistent with this result, both men who have the best mobility chances within their own company and men who perceive good chances to earn more elsewhere were more likely than others to express dissatisfaction with the prospect of remaining below comparison persons in earnings.

There were, however, some important unanticipated results

which show that our initial formulation of the relation between mobility chances and comparisons was inadequate. We found that mobility chances *within* the company and mobility chances *outside* the company had opposite effects on the choice of *presently* dissonant comparisons and on present satisfaction with comparisons. The men who had the best mobility chances within Atlas were those in the training program. Those men, by comparing upward less often and by choosing men of different status when they did compare upward, chose fewer presently dissonant comparisons than did men who were barred from the training program. Moreover, those in the training program are presently somewhat more satisfied with upward comparisons than are men barred from the program. When we considered mobility chances outside the company, however, we found that men with the best mobility chances were more likely than others to choose comparison persons who earn more than themselves and to be presently dissatisfied with the comparisons they made.

The explanation of these seemingly contradictory results appears to lie in the fact that there are some important practical and conceptual differences in the two measures of "mobility chances" which were used. Having the best mobility chances within the company means that one is assured (through the training program) of aid and encouragement in advancing in rank and wages as rapidly as possible. The best way for such men to maximize their chances for advancement is to stay where they are, work hard, and wait. Such men have no incentive to protest their present position and to argue for a higher status. If, as we have inferred from previous data, dissonant comparisons may serve as a protest against one's present status, then it is understandable why men in the training program did not often choose dissonant comparisons.

Having good mobility chances outside the company constitutes a very different situation. It means, on the one hand, that a man may find a better job somewhere else and, on the other hand, that he is in a good bargaining position to ask for more at

Atlas. In either case, the mobility chances which are inherent in having the chance to earn more elsewhere can be realized, not by staying put and keeping quiet, but by actively fighting for a raise.

It seems likely, therefore, that those with good mobility chances outside the company would be motivated to protest their present status and to claim a higher status. That such men should often choose dissonant comparisons is consistent with our interpretation that such comparisons may serve as a protest against one's present status and as a justification for advancement.

We may conclude from our data that it is not the excellence of mobility chances as such which has a crucial influence on the choice of comparisons. The important factor appears to be whether assured, legitimated paths for advancement have been provided for those who feel they deserve advancement. Where men have good mobility chances of this type, we may expect them typically to choose presently *consonant* comparisons and to be presently *satisfied* with the comparisons they choose. However, where men's mobility chances consist in a strategic economic bargaining position, where advancement has to be fought for and won, we may expect good mobility chances to lead to the choice of presently *dissonant* comparisons and to present *dissatisfaction* with comparisons.

9.4. Personal Responsibility

We predicted that men who see the responsibility for their occupational position as *not* being their own will be likely to choose dissonant wage comparisons and to be dissatisfied with comparisons. In line with these hypotheses we expected that men who reject personal responsibility would compare upward (to those who earn more than themselves) more often than others. This prediction was not supported by the data.

However, among men who are likely for other reasons to choose upward comparisons (i.e., those who stand relatively low on pay and those who have been barred from the company training program) perceptions of personal responsibility made a big difference in the *type* of upward comparison chosen and in satisfaction with such comparisons. Men who stand relatively low on pay and who *reject* responsibility for their fate chose upward comparisons at their own occupational level (i.e., dissonant upward comparisons) more often than did low-earners who *accept* personal responsibility for their position. Those who stand relatively low on pay and who reject responsibility for this position are also more likely than other low-earners to be dissatisfied with upward comparisons. Similarly, men who have been barred from the training program and who reject personal responsibility for this position are more often dissatisfied with upward comparisons than are those men who are barred from the program but who accept responsibility for their position.

Thus, although the degree of acceptance of personal responsibility does not in itself greatly affect the choice of comparisons, it serves to accentuate or blunt the effect of other forces. A situation of earning less than others like oneself or of being barred from the training program can have far different meanings, depending on who is responsible for one's position. Where a man accepts personal responsibility, he has no justification for protesting a poor wage position and therefore less motivation for making dissonant comparisons. Where a man blames his misfortunes on others, the choice of dissonant comparisons can serve to bolster his claim for higher status.

9.5. Social Influences

We expected that men who are told by others that they deserve to earn more will be likely to choose dissonant comparisons and to be dissatisfied with comparisons. The available measure of such social influences was subject to contamination by respondents' own ideas about their wages. Our results using this measure must, therefore, be interpreted cautiously. However, the available data generally support the predictions made. Men exposed to social influences which define their position as too low were likely to choose comparison persons who earn more than themselves, regardless of their relative pay position, as objectively measured. Men who report strong social influences defining their position as inappropriately low were also more likely to choose dissonant upward comparisons who are of similar status (in occupational level and place of work) as themselves.

There is some evidence, however, that others' opinions about a man's wage position will influence his comparisons only if he objectively stands moderate or high relative to others like himself. In such cases, where a man is objectively doing fairly well, the opinion of others that he deserves even more makes him more likely to choose dissonant comparisons. However, when a man's objective position relative to others is low, he is likely to choose dissonant comparisons regardless of what others say to him. The data show also that where others say that a man deserves more, he is more likely to be dissatisfied with the comparisons he chose.

The effect on comparisons of the "social reality" that one is doing more poorly than appropriate is, thus, similar to the effect on comparisons of the objective reality that one is doing poorly relative to those of like status. In both cases, men are likely to be confronted with cases of dissonant comparisons. Moreover, the perceptual prominence of such dissonant comparisons will make men feel that they deserve to earn more, and is thus likely to produce the motivation to fight for a higher status. Both in their perceptual effects and in their motivational effects, then, low relative pay position, whether objectively defined or socially defined, is likely to lead to the choice of dissonant comparisons and to dissatisfaction with comparisons.

9.6. The Choice of Similar and Dissimilar Comparisons

The present data are pertinent to Festinger's inference that persons will tend to compare themselves to those who are not only similar to themselves on the dimension of comparison but who are also similar in other relevant attributes. In the present research, men were asked to choose comparisons whose earnings are *different* from their own. It could be argued that the necessity of choosing men with different earnings naturally led many men to choose comparison persons who are also of different status in other respects. Although there is truth in this argument, it is also true that men who chose upward comparisons of *different* general status differ in consistent and meaningful ways from men who chose upward comparisons of *similar* status.

Among men who stand relatively low on wages compared to others like themselves, those who accept personal responsibility for their low position were more likely to choose upward comparison persons of *higher* status than were those who reject personal responsibility. Such comparisons are consonant and are consistent with our expectation that men who accept responsibility will have more motivation to choose consonant comparisons.

We found also that men who are in the company training program were, when choosing comparison persons who earn more than themselves, significantly more likely than those barred from the program to choose persons of higher occupational status and different place of work. Such comparisons are consonant. Although we did not predict that men in the program would be likely to choose consonant comparisons, this result appears consistent with other findings which show that men who have no motivation to protest their present status are more likely than others to choose consonant comparisons.

It seems likely, therefore, that certain groups of persons, when their attention is turned to those who earn more than themselves, will purposely compare to those of *higher* general status in order to justify their own lower position on wages. We cannot, then, state categorically that men will always tend to choose comparisons of similar general status. Whether or not this will be true in any given case depends on the direction of comparison (i.e., whether the comparison person is earning more or less) and on the motivations of the comparer to choose consonant or dissonant comparisons.

9.7. Comparisons of Attributes Other Than Pay

Finally, a few words about the generalizability of these data and interpretations should be added. In considering the choice of *wage* comparisons, we have been dealing with an instance of comparisons of the amount of a social reward received. Other examples of social reward comparisons are comparisons of prestige, of popularity, of rank, of affection, and of material goods. It seems likely that the findings reported here are generally applicable to comparisons of these other social rewards. However, there are other types of comparisons which appear to differ in important ways from comparisons of social rewards. These types include comparisons of personal qualities (e.g., size, athletic skill, initiative) and of opinions. Careful theoretical analysis and empirical work will be required to discover the extent to which the present findings apply also to these other types of comparisons.

RESPONSE DISTRIBUTIONS NOT REPORTED ELSEWHERE

Comparisons to Persons Who Earn More Than Respondent *

A. Which of these statements best shows how you feel about the way your earnings now compare to his earnings?	Number of Comparisons
1. I am *very satisfied* with the way my earnings now compare to his earnings	58
2. I am *satisfied* with the way my earnings now compare to his earnings	279
3. I am *neither satisfied nor dissatisfied* with the way my earnings now compare to his earnings	113
4. I am *not too satisfied* with the way my earnings now compare to his earnings	75
5. I am *not at all satisfied* with the way my earnings now compare to his earnings	28
Total	553

* Each respondent spontaneously chose from zero to two comparison persons who earn more than himself.

B. Thinking of what he is earning now, suppose you   Number of
   never made as much as that—how would you feel?   Comparisons [†]

1. I would still feel very satisfied	34
2. I would feel satisfied	215
3. I would feel neither satisfied nor dissatisfied	84
4. I would feel not too satisfied	76
5. I would feel not at all satisfied	38
6. No answer	3

                                                      Total   450

Comparisons to Persons Who Earn Less Than Respondent [‡]

A. SUMMARY CODE: Occupational Level of   Number of
   Comparison Person   Comparisons

1. Professional	28
2. Proprietor of own business; manager	19
3. Clerical or sales	26
4. Foreman (blue-collar supervisory)	14
5. Blue-collar non-supervisory: skilled and semi-skilled, including skilled and semi-skilled service workers	245
6. Unskilled labor: including unskilled service workers	29
7. Unemployed	0

[†] Only respondents who refrained from expressing dissatisfaction about presently earning less than the comparison person were asked this question. Each respondent spontaneously chose from zero to two comparison persons who earn more than himself.

[‡] Each respondent spontaneously chose from zero to two comparison persons who earn less than himself.

8. Farm owner or farm worker   **11**

9. Blue-collar: NA supervisory, skilled or un-skilled   **12**

10. R does not mention occupational level; R does not know this person's occupation   **14**

Total   **398**

B. SUMMARY CODE: Is comparison person a close relative of R?   Number of Comparisons

1. Yes: Indicates that comparison person is close relative   **126**

2. Possibly: Work mentioned is same as any job of brother or brother-in-law mentioned in later question   **27**

3. No: Indicates that comparison person is *not* a close relative or does not indicate relationship to comparison person *and* no coincidence of occupation with brother or brother-in-law   **245**

Total   **398**

C. SUMMARY CODE: Does comparison person work at Atlas?   Number of Comparisons

1. Yes: R indicates that comparison person works at Atlas   **51**

2. No: R indicates that comparison person does *not* work at Atlas   **246**

3. No indication where comparison person works; R does not know where comparison figure works   **101**

Total   **398**

D. Which of these statements best shows how you feel about the way your earnings now compare to his earnings?

Number of Comparisons

(Responses chosen from card given to respondent)

1. I am *very satisfied* with the way my earnings now compare to his earnings   151

2. I am satisfied with the way my earnings now compare to his earnings   185

3. I am *neither satisfied nor dissatisfied* with the way my earnings now compare to his earnings   47

4. I am *not too satisfied* with the way my earnings now compare to his earnings   12

5. I am *not at all* satisfied with the way my earnings now compare to his earnings   1

6. No answer   2

Total   398

E. Could you tell me why you feel that way?

Number of Responses [§]

ADVANTAGES ENJOYED BY R

1. Financial advantage—mere fact of earning more   155

2. Financial advantage—uses for money   20

3. Non-financial advantages   89

REASONS WHY R IS EARNING MORE

4. R's job requires more; R is better trained   47

5. R has more seniority, experience, is older   24

[§] A maximum of two answers for each respondent concerning each comparison were coded for this question.

6. R has shown good or better personal qualities, judgment   6

WAYS IN WHICH COMPARISON PERSON QUALIFIES FOR (BUT DOES NOT RECEIVE) EARNINGS AS MUCH OR MORE THAN R

7. Comparison person's job requires as much or more; comparison person is equally or better trained   48

8. Comparison person has as much or more seniority, experience; is as old or older   7

9. R is not interested in comparing earnings   30

10. Other, not codable above   63

11. No answer   10

Total   499

Perception of Personal Responsibility [II]

A. For men who grew up when you did, how much would you say a man's chances for getting ahead in life depended on himself and how much on things beyond his control?	Number of Men Making Response
(One of following responses chosen from a card)	
1. *Almost entirely* on the man himself	136
2. *Mostly* on the man himself	255
3. *Somewhat* on the man himself	82
4. *Very little* on the man himself	15
5. *Not at all* on the man himself	0
6. No answer	1
Total	489

[II] The construction of an index of acceptance of personal responsibility, using the two items shown here, is described in Chapter III.

B. Thinking about Atlas, how much would you say advancement usually depends on how well a man can do a job and how much on other things?

Number of Men Making Response

(One of following responses chosen from a card)

1. *Almost entirely* on how well a man can do a job		75
2. *Mostly* on how well a man can do a job		232
3. *Somewhat* on how well a man can do a job		131
4. *Very little* on how well a man can do a job		36
5. *Not at all* on how well a man can do a job		12
6. No answer		3
	Total	489

APPENDIX B

PAY RATE DISTRIBUTION

Hourly Pay Rates (dollars)	Number of Men
1.77	17
1.88	21
1.98	43
2.09	63
2.21	62
2.34	80
2.48	157
2.62	18
2.74	28
Total	489

METHODOLOGICAL NOTE

Differences Among Respondents in Number of Upward Comparisons Made

A special methodological problem was presented in this study by the fact that each respondent was permitted spontaneously to chose two comparison persons without regard to whether or not these comparison persons earn more or less than himself. In these circumstances, some respondents chose no upward comparisons (persons who earn more than themselves), some respondents chose one upward comparison, and some respondents chose two upward comparisons. In considering the upward comparisons of any given category of respondents, therefore, data were available on two comparisons for some respondents and on only one comparison for other respondents. To have included information about each upward comparison of each respondent would have given additional weighting to the respondents who made *two* upward comparisons and lesser weight to those who made only *one* upward comparison.

However, since we usually wished to test the statistical significance of differences among groups of *men*, not among groups of comparisons, it was desirable to give each respondent equal weight in the tables. In order to accomplish this, the following procedures were used:

Satisfaction, Both Present and Potential, with Upward Comparisons. Where a respondent expressed his feelings of satisfaction con-

120

cerning two comparisons, an average score based on the two responses was calculated, thus giving him a single score comparable to the score of a respondent who chose only one upward comparison.

Occupational Level of Upward Comparison Persons. Where various groups of respondents were being compared according to the occupational level of the comparisons they chose, only the first codable comparison person chosen by any single respondent was included in the tables. Where comparisons to persons at various occupational levels were being contrasted, according to the degree of satisfaction they elicited, only one choice per respondent in any given occupational level was included in the tables.

Place of Work of Upward Comparison Persons. Where various groups of respondents were being compared according to the place of work of the comparison persons they chose, only the first codable comparison person chosen by any single respondent was included in the tables. Where comparisons to persons working at the company were being contrasted with comparisons to persons working outside the company, according to the degree of satisfaction they elicited, only the first comparison to someone at Atlas and the first comparison to someone outside Atlas were included in the tables.

Family Relation of Upward Comparison Persons. Where comparisons to persons who are close relatives were being contrasted with comparisons to persons who are not close relatives, according to the degree of satisfaction they elicited, only the first comparison to a close relative and the first comparison to a non-relative was included in the tables.

Reasons for Satisfaction or Dissatisfaction with Comparisons. Where the reasons given by those satisfied with upward comparisons were listed, the reasons given by any respondent concerning only the first comparison with which he is satisfied were included in the tables. Similarly, the answers of any respondent concerning only the first comparison with which he is dissatisfied were included in the tables.

BIBLIOGRAPHY

1. Cooley, C. H., *Human Nature and the Social Order,* New York: Charles Scribner's Sons, 1902.

2. Chapman, D. W., and Volkmann, J., "A social determinant of the level of aspiration," *J. Abnorm. Soc. Psychol.,* 1939, **34,** 225–238.

3. Durkheim, E., *Suicide,* Paris: F. Alcan, 1897.

4. ———. *The Elementary Forms of Religious Life,* Paris: F. Alcan, 1912.

5. Festinger, L., A theory of social comparison processes, in *Small Groups,* A. Hare, E. Borgata, and R. Bales eds., New York: Alfred A. Knopf, Inc., 1955, 163–187.

6. ———. *A Theory of Cognitive Dissonance,* Evanston, Ill.: Row, Peterson and Co., 1957.

7. Hilgard, E. R., Sait, E. M., and Magaret, G. A., "Level of aspiration as affected by relative standing in an experimental social group," *J. Exp. Psychol.,* 1940, **27,** 411–421.

8. Hyman, H., "The psychology of status," *Arch. Psychol.,* 1942, **38,** 15.

9. Kaplan, N., *Reference group theory and voting behavior,* unpublished doctoral dissertation, Columbia Univ., 1955.

10. Kelley, H. H., Two functions of reference groups; in *Readings in Social Psychology,* rev. ed., eds. G. Swanson, T. M. Newcomb, and E. L. Hartley, New York: Henry Holt & Co., Inc., 1952.

11. McIntosh, A., "Differential effect of the status of the competing group on levels of aspiration," *Amer. J. Psychol.,* 1942, **55,** 546–554.

12. Mead, G. H., *Mind, Self, and Society,* Chicago, Ill.: University of Chicago Press, 1934.

13. Merton, R. K., and Kitt, A., Contributions to the theory of reference group behavior, in *Continuities in Social Research: Studies in the Scope and Methods of "The American Soldier,"* eds. R. K. Merton and P. F. Lazarsfeld, Glencoe, Ill.: The Free Press, 1950.

14. Newcomb, T. M., *Personality and Social Change: Attitude Formation in a Student Community*, New York: Dryden Press, 1943.

15. Sherif, M., "A study of some social factors in perception," *Arch. Psychol.*, 1935, No. 187.

16. ———. *The Psychology of Social Norms*, New York: Harper & Brothers, Publishers, 1936.

17. Stern, E., and Keller, S., "Spontaneous group references in France," *Publ. Opin. Quart.*, 1953, **17**, 208–217.

18. Stouffer, S. A., *et al.*, *The American Soldier*. Vols. I and II of *Studies in Social Psychology in World War II*. Princeton, N.J.: Princeton University Press, 1949–50.

19. Sumner, W. G., *Folkways*. Boston: Ginn and Company, 1906.

20. Turner, R. H., "Reference groups of future-oriented men," *Soc. Forces*, 1955, **34**, 130–136.